Fifteen Days in September that Will Change the World

FIFTEEN DAYS
IN
SEPTEMBER

THAT WILL CHANGE THE WORLD

MARK S. HOFFMEISTER

Fifteen Days in September that Will Change the World

ISBN-13: 978-1511849340

DEDICATION

This book is dedicated to my father,

Arthur Frederick Hoffmeister

ACKNOWLEDGEMENTS

I am grateful to Rob Fischer for editing this book for me. He challenged me on many of my ideas and conclusions. And even though he may not agree with everything I've written, he applied himself diligently to helping me with this book. I also appreciate Heather Wilbur whose creative work graces the cover.

I would also like to thank my wife Kelly for her constant support during the time it took to write this book. Kelly has been a blessing to me and without her steadfast encouragement I would not have been able to complete this book.

As always, I am thankful for the support of my children who have told me many times that I need to continue with my writing. Many thanks to each of you.

TABLE OF CONTENTS

Chapter One

OUR PERPLEXING TIMES

Do you ever get the feeling that something is just not right; that things happening in the world today are disturbing and unsettling? Do events that appear in the news make you think that the world is becoming unhinged, or that people are routinely exhibiting behavior that can best be described as bizarre? Are you surprised when anomalous incidents seem to be occurring routinely and with ever increasing frequency?

If you feel that way you are not alone. We are living in some unusual times; and frequently the things unfolding around us can be frightening and disheartening. We are living in a time when even mundane events such as the weather seem to be fighting against us. Prolonged droughts are now commonplace, and when the rain comes we are not greeted with calm and refreshing relief—but rather with an onslaught of rain that pummels us with ferocity. The winter months settle in, and we are buried in mountains of snow that have accumulated by storm after storm after storm—all accompanied by numbing cold that penetrates to the bone. All too frequently, the weather is no longer something to be enjoyed, but rather something to be endured.

The stock market is as schizophrenic as the weather. Extreme fluctuations in the value of the market are now common, with wild panic causing drastic plunges in the Dow, and irrational exuberance causing an unexpected rise in the value of stocks. Longtime financial institutions are going out of business, and the threat of another fifty per cent drop in the stock market is looming on the horizon as a huge debt bubble hangs over us like a financial harbinger warning of impending doom.

All around us things are changing. Wars start unexpectedly and soon escalate out of control. Terrorist groups form and soon wreak havoc on those around them. Bizarre events are being recorded all around the world, from massive animal die-offs, to unusual sounds, tremendous explosive type noises, and unexplained apparitions in the skies over the earth. Even the nighttime skies are filled with portents of disaster as blood moons hint of ominous times in our near future.

Things seem to be escalating out of control on every front, with each day bringing more and more accounts of disturbing news. Sometimes we just want to retreat into our homes, and filter out the perplexing and vexing events around us. We all want security, but should we dismiss these things and pretend they are not happening just for our peace of mind?

Whether we want to acknowledge it or not, we are entering a period of time that God's Word characterizes as the end times. Things are not going to be "normal" like we have always known them for much longer. The circumstances all around us are going to be changing, and rather than ignoring these changes, we need to be recognizing these changes for what they are.

The Lord has not left us uninformed about the changes that are going to happen. He has filled His Word with detailed descriptions of what we can expect when the end times come upon us.

It comes as no surprise that the Lord has told us in detail what we can expect in these troubling times. The problem is that these details are contained in the "prophetic" sections of the Bible; and prophesy is for the most part being ignored by the churches today. We spend all of our time talking about other subjects in the Bible, all of which are necessary and good, but we spend practically no time talking about the sections of the Bible that give us thorough descriptions of what we can expect in the near future. We are told specifically in God's Word what we are to do to survive and thrive in these times, and how we are to act when we find ourselves in these circumstances.

The Bible spends a significant amount of time describing end time events. But all too frequently we pretend they don't really exist, and act as if there's nothing to worry about.

We can't ignore the prophetic message of the Bible any longer—especially the portions that deal with end time events. We shouldn't be scared of them, we should be open to the prophetic sections and study them so we can know what to expect when things start to happen. If we don't start talking about these things, then others will define the Bible message for us—and the message will be whatever they say it is, instead of a message that has been carefully detailed and laid out in God's Word.

If we continue to ignore the prophetic sections of the Bible, the church is going to lose its voice when the world calls out for answers. We will no longer be the source of sound and compelling doctrine based on extensive research from the Bible. Instead, we will degenerate into carefully crafted sound bites telling people what they want to hear. We will be another source of "fluff" that neither satisfies nor answers the deeper questions surrounding the events that will soon come to pass. We need to be immersed in deep and compelling research based on what God's Word actually says, using the Bible to interpret other sections of the Bible that we don't understand. Only then we will be a resource to others that can calm troubled souls, and speak peace and understanding when chaos and disorder reign.

With this in mind, we are faced with a perplexing dichotomy. In the time when Jesus walked the earth, the Jewish people wanted a conquering king to come and free them from the tyranny of Roman oppression. What they received instead was a message of love. In our time, we concentrate solely on the message of love, and forget that a Conquering King is coming back to the earth to right the wrongs that have been committed, and to set up His Kingdom on the earth. The Age of Grace that has been so prevalent in God's dealings with our world is going to be replaced by the time of judgment—and this is something we are not prepared for.

The primary example of this is the description of war concerning the nation of Israel contained in the pages of the Bible. But even when discussing end time wars, we in the church cannot agree on what God's Word is saying. Is there one big war, or are there several end time wars described in the Bible? How can we know which view is right?

Many people rightly believe that when the end times come upon us, there will be a terrible war in Israel where the nations of the world gather massive armies to annihilate God's chosen people at Armageddon. Many say that Armageddon will be the mother of all battles, the one battle that is described in the Bible that is the climactic battle of all time. They see Armageddon as the one battle that fulfills all that has been written about the nations and peoples that come against Israel; the one battle that settles everything that has been written about those who choose to fight against God.

While the Battle of Armageddon is truly a climactic battle, and a battle where Christ will be completely victorious in settling the affairs of the world; it is not the only battle that is described in the Bible that sets the stage and initiates end-time events. Are all of God's prophecies encapsulated in this one battle, or are there biblical patterns and precedents that suggest there is more than one battle in Israel's future? If there is a biblical pattern and precedent that suggests otherwise, how do we discern this pattern from all the biblical prophecies that speak of end-time events? How can we make sense out of the maze of Scriptures that describe the fate of nations that fight against Israel?

Many Bible teachers and scholars have overcome this problem by wrapping the fates of all these nations and peoples into one battle, the Battle of Armageddon. After all, if this is the final decisive battle, then everything must be concluded in this battle; and all Scriptures must apply to this one battle. While this is reasonable and sound thinking, there are clues sprinkled throughout God's Word that would suggest otherwise. Is there a biblical pattern contained in the Scriptures that we can discover with some detailed research that will show us how many wars there will be leading up to the ultimate triumph of Israel?

The Biblical Pattern for Israel's End Time Wars

There is just such a pattern in God's Word. It's not a secret, you don't need any specialized knowledge to discern it, and it's there for all to see with careful study of God's Word. It's based on a pattern imbedded in the Scriptures long ago, and it's the key for understanding the events that are going to happen in the future. We can begin to discover the pattern when we look at past events in Israel, during the time when they began to lose the land God had set aside for them. The nation that had embraced God, and reached their zenith in the times of King David and King Solomon, turned away from God and plunged into the spiral of defeat that would lead to the loss of their nation and the scattering of their people throughout the world.

Ancient Israel lost their nation, and **the pattern by which they lost their country will be the pattern by which they will regain their nation** and fulfill their prophetic destiny. If we are going to discover this pattern, then we have to examine what happened to all of the twelve tribes of Israel, and how Israel ceased being a nation. If we are going to gain insight into how things will play out in the end-time events, we will let this pattern be the template for how Israel will ultimately be victorious in the coming years. In essence, we will let events of the biblical past be our key to unlocking the events that will shortly come to pass in the future. By doing this, the events that God has in store for Israel will become clearer to us and we can make sense of the maze of Scriptures that determines the fate of many nations.

We will have a very simple set of rules for doing this. We will let the Bible interpret the Bible. We will base our conclusions on what the Bible says and on the biblical patterns we find in God's Word. That way we can eliminate our own prejudices and pre-conceived ideas and let God's Word speak for itself.

If we are going to make any sense out of all the Scriptures that speak of the destiny of Israel as a nation, and of the wars leading to that destiny, then we need to begin in the past and look at the specific time in Israel's history when the Jewish people had rejected God. Because of their rebellion, the Lord let their nation fail and be broken apart...and thus began the fall of ancient Israel.

The Fall of Ancient Israel

In order to see how God will accomplish His will, perhaps we should ask ourselves the following question: Did ancient Israel fall all at once in one battle, or was there more than one war leading to their demise as a nation? For our intents and purposes, we are not going to examine everything that led up to the fall of ancient Israel, but rather examine the process by which they were destroyed as a nation.

Ancient Israel had split into two nations following the death of Solomon, the son of David. One nation consisted of Samaria, or ten of the tribes of Israel. The other nation included the tribes of Judah and Benjamin and was centered on the capitol city of Jerusalem. Both nations had a common enemy in the Assyrians, a vicious enemy that was ruthlessly conquering everyone around them.

The fall of the nation of Israel began when the ten tribes were conquered by the Assyrian leader Shalmaneser when he laid siege to Samaria. The siege lasted three years, started by the Assyrian King Shalmaneser (2 Kings 17: 4-6), and finished by the Assyrian King Sargon II in 722 BC when Samaria was defeated.[1] This was the first war of destruction that led to the demise of the nation of Israel. The Assyrians took many captives from the ten tribes and hauled them away to Assyria (2 Kings 17:6). Thus the destruction of the nation of Israel began with a war that resulted in the loss of Samaria (the ten tribes). This was the first war.

---

1   *Ancient History Encyclopedia,* "Sargon II," by Joshua J. Mark, July 3, 2014, *http://www.ancient.eu/Sargon.II/.*

A little over twenty years later, the Assyrians under a new leader named Sennacherib, came to finish the job of the destruction of Israel. They had their sights on Judah and the capitol city of Jerusalem. Sennacherib brought a tremendous army of 185,000 men with him. He laid siege to the city of Jerusalem and demanded the surrender of the Jewish people. Sennacherib left while awaiting their surrender and went to another battle, but his army remained around the city of Jerusalem.

An amazing thing happened when the King of Judah named Hezekiah realized the predicament of the Jewish people and turned to God for help. He repented of all his sins, and then implored all the people of Jerusalem to repent and turn back to God. The people listened to Hezekiah, humbled themselves, and turned away from the things that were alienating them from God. When the Jewish people, surrounded by the massive army of Sennacherib, did this, God heard their prayers and moved to save His people surrounded in Jerusalem. The Lord used supernatural intervention (heavenly intervention, something not caused by the hand of man) to destroy the army of Sennacherib in one night. The army of 185,000 men was all destroyed by the Lord in one night by an angel of the Lord, and in the morning they were all dead corpses. (Isaiah 37:7, 36)

This was the second war in which Israel was attacked, and this war also sets a precedent for what is going to happen in the future. God intervened on Israel's behalf using supernatural means to prevent the slaughter of the Jewish people. The second war ended when God intervened to destroy the invading army.

The third and final war in the destruction of Israel as a nation began when a new power arrived on the scene. The Babylonians under the leadership of Nebuchadnezzar invaded the land of Israel and laid siege to the capitol city of Jerusalem. This time the

Jewish people did not turn back to God and were destroyed by Nebuchadnezzar and carried off into the land of Babylon in 586 BC. (2 Kings 24:11-14; 25:1-7)

In this third war, God clearly orchestrated the destruction of Jerusalem and the rise of Nebuchadnezzar as the agent of His destruction (2 Kings 24:3-4). Nebuchadnezzar had a dream given to him that the prophet Daniel was called on to interpret (Daniel 2:31-35) and was aided in many different ways in his historic destiny by God. (Daniel 2: 37). Nebuchadnezzar was an ordained agent of God set apart to accomplish his appointed destiny.

At the end of this third war, the nation of Israel was broken up and ceased being a nation. Thus, the powerful nation of Israel was not destroyed with just one war; it took a series of three wars to lead to their ultimate destruction. Going back to the original question then, we now have an answer to how many wars it took to destroy the nation of Israel as a functioning country in ancient times. It was a series of three wars that led to their destruction. These three wars set a precedent and pattern that we should look for in the future wars that will involve Israel.

Why is this number of three wars so important?

It's important because it sets a biblical precedent and pattern that God uses to accomplish His purposes. Throughout the Bible God has used biblical patterns and precedents to carry out His will. For example, Jacob and his twelve sons, the nation of Israel, went into Egypt to avoid destruction by a famine, and Jesus as a small child was taken into Egypt by Mary and Joseph to avoid destruction by Herod, who wanted to kill him. This established a clear biblical pattern.

We find another biblical pattern in the story of the Israelites as they were wandering in the desert. Venomous snakes came among them and began biting and killing many of the Israelites. How did God tell Moses to solve this problem? He told Moses to make a fiery serpent and place it on a pole, and all those who were bitten could look upon it and be saved from death (Numbers 21:8). This was peculiar advice on how to survive a snake bite, but not bizarre when you realize this was a biblical pattern and was symbolic of Jesus on the cross. All who look to Jesus as their Savior are saved.

Another biblical pattern can be found while Moses was leading the Israelites to the Promised Land. They found themselves in an inhospitable desert with no water. The people of Israel were thirsty, and Moses was instructed by God to strike a rock (symbolic of Jesus, 1 Corinthians 10:4) to provide water for the people. When he struck the Rock as he had been instructed, water gushed forth out of the rock (Exodus 17:6). This was symbolic of the biblical pattern where Jesus would be stricken for His people and die when He came the first time. However, when the people were thirsty a second time, Moses was instructed to speak to another rock and it would bring forth water (Numbers 20:8). Moses did not listen to what God had told him, and instead struck the rock, a clear violation of what the Lord had instructed him to do that led to a violation of the biblical pattern when Jesus would come again the second time as a conquering King and would not be stricken. The second time when He comes again, He will listen to the voice of His people asking Him to come back for them so He can protect them from their enemies. This violation of the biblical pattern was so egregious to God that Moses was prevented from entering the Promised Land because he did not recognize the pattern and did not do as God instructed. (Numbers 20:11-12) Christ will not be struck the second time when he returns, but will be the Conquering King, and the Lion of the tribe of Judah (Revelation 5:5).

God takes biblical patterns very seriously. Moses' failure to obey the Lord and comply with the biblical pattern led to him not being able to enter the Promised Land. This might seem like a minor infraction to us, but to God it was very serious to violate a biblical pattern that he had established for all of us to recognize. Biblical patterns and precedents are there for us to see so we can gain insight into the way that God accomplishes His purposes. They are there for our instruction and as a way to lead us to God. It is a rare way to get a glimpse into the mind of God. If we fail to notice the biblical pattern, then we may fail to see how God is going to do something that He has said He would do.

With this in mind, let's now apply the biblical pattern set forth in the destruction of Israel as a nation in the past, to the future wars in Israel that will lead to accomplishment of Israel's prophetic destiny.

Chapter Two

THE ESTABLISHMENT WARS OF MODERN ISRAEL

Israel was established as a nation again by a vote in the United Nations on May 14th, 1948, and was immediately engulfed in a war fighting for its survival the very next day. The combined nations of Egypt, Syria, Iraq and Lebanon attacked to prevent the re-establishment of the Jewish people in the land and to prevent the fledgling nation from ever taking root. The attack from these countries began the War of Independence for Israel. It lasted for ten months and officially ended on the 10th of March, 1949. This was a war for the establishment of the nation, and when it ended the Jewish people had the land they had been granted by the United Nations, and 60 percent of the land in the partition plan of the attacking Arab countries.

The map on the following page shows the projected boundaries for the state of Palestine proposed by the United Nations prior to the War of Independence. The Jewish people chose the name of Israel for their nation and controlled much of the area shown at the end of the war with the exception of the Golan Heights, near

Syria, the West Bank west of the Dead Sea, the city of Jerusalem, and the Gaza strip near Egypt.

This was the first War in the re-establishment of Israel as a nation, the first war where the Jewish people used all of their resources and repelled an attack that wanted to destroy them as a nation.

The Second War

The second war where the nation of Israel was fighting for its life was called the Six Day War. Israel had noted significant preparation by the army of Egypt to launch an all-out offensive to destroy their nation in June of 1967. Israel launched a pre-emptive strike to prevent this catastrophic attack. The tiny nation of Israel soon found itself standing against the combined armies of the nations of Egypt, Syria, Jordan and Iraq. Again they were fighting for their lives and the survival of their country.

In what can only be described as a miracle, Israel prevailed against overwhelming odds and defeated the combined armies of the nations trying to destroy them. They accomplished this feat in just six days from June 5th through June 10th of 1967.

Israel was able to regain a significant amount of land in this war and controlled more of the land that they had controlled in ancient times including the Golan Heights, the West Bank, the Gaza strip, and the Sinai peninsula.

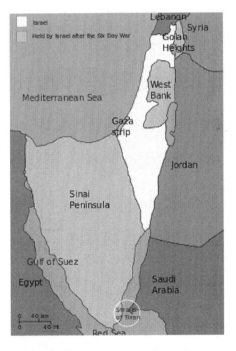

While Israel controlled more land at the conclusion of the Six Day War, these were not the boundaries that the Lord had in mind when he originally granted Israel their land in ancient times. A careful examination of the Scriptures reveals that this was not how God envisioned the nation of Israel. In Genesis, God describes the boundaries that He granted the nation of Israel. It says, "In the same day the Lord made a covenant with Abram, saying, 'Unto thy seed have I given this land, from the river of Egypt, unto the great river, the river Euphrates.'" (Genesis 15:18) This was not a suggestion on the size of their country, it was a solemn promise of what their borders would be some day.

If we truly want to see how God envisioned and proclaimed the nation of Israel, then we need to see exactly what He is saying in His Word. God did not see the nation of Israel as a small nation with the territories captured at the end of the Six Day War, but as a nation stretching from the "river of Egypt," which is the Nile River, to the Euphrates River. The Euphrates River extends from northern Syria through the nation of Iraq, down to the Persian Gulf. It is an area far greater than what is now the nation of Israel. If we examine what the Lord has said in His land grant to the nation of Israel, then the future nation of Israel will be comprised of land composing the nations of Lebanon, Syria, Iraq, Jordan, and parts of the nations of Saudi Arabia and Egypt.

What God has said should be the borders of the nation of Israel is significantly larger than the tiny nation we see today and is clearly larger than the territory captured in the Six Day War. The nation of Israel grew significantly at the conclusion of that war, but it was still far from what God had envisioned for His people.

The second war in the establishment of Israel as a nation came to a conclusion. The Jewish people had been victorious yet again in an all-out war to destroy them as a nation. The third war against them would come on their holiest day of the year, and would catch the nation of Israel unprepared.

The Third War

Two wars had established Israel as a nation, with surprising victories and additions of land to their territory, but the third war would not go as smoothly as the first two. It came on Yom Kippur in 1973, when many of Israel's fighting men were home with their families to celebrate the holiest day of their year. The Jewish people were caught off guard when the combined forces of Egypt, Syria, Jordan and Iraq launched a surprise attack to annihilate them and destroy their nation. It began on October 6th and lasted until October 25th of 1973.

During that time the Israeli Defensive Forces (IDF) fought bravely to repel the nations that were bent on their destruction. They suffered tremendous losses, but in the end they were able to successfully repel the invading forces and maintained control of most of the areas they had previously gained.

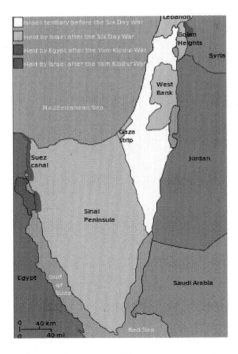

At the conclusion of the Yom Kippur War in 1973, Israel was basically in the same position as it was before the war. It had gained and lost very little additional territory, and was still far from the nation that God had envisioned.

Since that time, Israel has been steadily losing territory that it had gained in these three wars because of the demands of the United Nations. The world has been demanding "land for peace," and has been consistently carving up the nation of Israel and telling the Jewish people that they will have peace and security if only they give up the lands captured in the first two wars. Israel has acquiesced to the demands of other nations and relinquished control of the Sinai and Gaza strip, but have gained neither security nor peace. In fact, Israel's position has become even more tenuous in recent years and the Jewish state has been enduring an almost constant state of war and unceasing attacks from its neighbors.

This now leads us to the point where Israel finds itself today. They fought three wars for the establishment of their nation, and now they stand on the edge of a precipice, surrounded on every side by nations that want to destroy them and have tried to do so on many occasions. God's promises to the nation of Israel loom on the horizon, and the aggression of other nations toward Israel will soon be dealt with in exactly the way God said He would handle it. The template is contained in the Bible. The fate of the nations that continue to try to destroy God's chosen people and His chosen land has already been decided and will soon be carried out. God's patience and tolerance of sin will not continue indefinitely. A change is coming. A biblical pattern will soon reassert itself and the prophesied wars in Israel's future will soon come to pass.

The hint that things will soon be occurring is being written in a place for all to see...it is being displayed in a place where everyone can see for themselves...it is being written in the heavens above us.

Chapter Three

SIGNS IN THE HEAVENS

God is sending us a message and it's written in the heavens above. This may sound like hyperbole until we again look at what has happened in the past and take notice of the biblical pattern and precedent that the Lord has created. It all began with the re-establishment of Israel as a nation. As you recall, when Israel was once again declared a nation in May of 1948, it was immediately enveloped in a war for survival. The war lasted for ten months and ended in March of 1949. A very curious thing happened in 1949, and was displayed in the skies for all to see.

The following phenomenon appeared in the night sky:

A blood moon formed in the night skies over the earth. What exactly is a blood moon? A blood moon is caused by a total lunar eclipse when the earth passes between the sun and the moon. This blocks the light reflecting off the moon's surface and causes some of the sun's rays to curve around the earth causing the moon to appear with a reddish hue. The vivid red appearance of the moon caused by the bending light is referred to as a blood red moon by NASA.

While a blood moon in itself is not that unusual, four blood moons occurring back to back is very unusual. This is referred to as a tetrad, and means there are four total lunar eclipses happening back to back, something that is very rare indeed. A tetrad had not occurred for 368 years, and now was manifesting again as the tiny nation of Israel was fighting for survival.[2] It seems that God was showing a sign in the night sky for all to see. You can learn more about the blood moon tetrad by reviewing the work of Pastor Mark Biltz, from El-Shaddai Ministries, and by reading the book by Pastor John Hagee entitled, *Four Blood Moons, Something is About to Change.*

During this first blood moon tetrad, Israel was engaged in a war for its survival and ended up gaining a significant amount of land. Could the blood moon tetrad be a sign and a precedent for what happened to Israel at the time of the tetrad's appearance?

Let's review the events at the time of the tetrad. Israel was involved in a war for survival and ended up defeating her enemies and gaining a significant amount of land. Israel was formed as a nation in 1948; and the tetrad appeared in 1949-1950. This is curious timing indeed, but can the timing really form a precedent for us to recognize? If that is the case, then a blood moon tetrad should form again during a time when Israel is at war, fighting for

---

2   http://eclipse.gsfc.nasa.gov/LEcat5/LE1501-1600.html

her life, and a time when Israel gains a significant amount of land. Did this scenario ever happen again?

It did happen indeed. Remember, a tetrad had not formed for 368 years until the formation of Israel as a nation. It was not going to be another 368 years until it happened again. Instead, another tetrad, another four blood moons, formed in the night skies in the years of 1967-1968, not even twenty years from the previous one. Coincidentally, at the time of the appearance, Israel was involved in another war fighting for her life—the Six Day War of June 1967. At the end of the Six Day War, Israel had gained the city of Jerusalem, the temple site, and a significant amount of land including the Golan Heights, the West Bank, the Gaza strip, and the Sinai Peninsula—all land that had been granted by God to Israel in Genesis.

It may seem astounding, but the tetrad's appearance again during a time of war, the Six Day War, may be impossible to ignore. Both times the tetrad or four blood moons manifested, the Jewish people were involved in a war and ended up gaining sizeable portions of land that had been granted to them by the Lord. Is this just a coincidence, or could the Lord be trying to show us something? Is there a biblical pattern or precedent here? If there is, then just what is the pattern God is trying to get us to see?

To answer these questions, we need to look at the third war in the establishment of Israel as a nation. This was the Yom Kippur war that took place in October of 1973. During this war, no tetrads or blood moons were seen. Israel was again fighting to prevent complete and total destruction of their country, and successfully repelled the invading forces of Egypt, Syria, Jordan and Iraq. What was different with this war? How did the Yom Kippur war differ from the War of Independence and the Six Day War? Why were no blood moons seen?

The answer to these questions deals with a matter of territory. In both the Israel War of Independence and the Six Day War, when the blood moon tetrad appeared, Israel gained a substantial amount of land that had been granted to them by the Lord. In Genesis, Abram was told that his promised seed was given the land "From the river of Egypt, unto the great river, the river Euphrates." (Genesis 15:18) Israel was able to gain some of this land in their first two wars, but not in the Yom Kippur War. In the Yom Kippur War, Israel was barely able to hang onto the land it had already captured, and lost some land it controlled near the Suez Canal.

It would appear that a biblical pattern or precedent has been set during the time of four blood moons occurring back to back (the tetrad). When this sign has been given in recent times, Israel has always been involved in a war for the survival of the Jewish people, a time when they faced overwhelming odds, and a time when they gained substantial amounts of territory in the land that God had previously granted them. Every time the tetrad has appeared, Israel has gained more land.

Will this pattern hold true in the future? Are there any more blood moon tetrads set to appear in the immediate future?

As I write this in January of 2015, a tetrad has already begun. The first two of the four blood moons have already appeared. This happened on April 15th, 2014, and October 8th, 2014. And what makes this tetrad even more amazing is that every one of these blood moons falls on a feast day for Israel as Pastor Mark Biltz has observed. The April 15th, 2014 blood moon fell on Passover, the first feast day for Israel, and the October 8th, 2014 blood moon fell on Succoth, or the feast of Tabernacles, on the last feast day for Israel in the year. The blood moons of 2015 will fall on Passover April 4th and Succoth on September 28th; again the first and last feast days in Israel. This makes the very rare appearance of a tetrad even rarer because each of the blood moons falls on a date that is highly significant to the Jewish people.

It's almost as if God is trying to highlight these dates so that everyone will take notice. Will the nations of the world see the blood moon signs and stop their interference in Israel? Or will these signs be ignored and the nations of the world continue to blindly insist that Israel give up portions of her country in order to obtain false promises of peace? Will we continue to go against what God has said should be the borders of Israel and continue the insanity of actively fighting against the will and wishes of God?

We will examine what this third series of four blood moons happening in 2014 and 2015 might mean. The implications of what is coming will be a *Transcendent Event*, an event that will eventually effect the lives of every man, woman and child on our planet. It will be difficult to understand unless we view things from God's perspective, and try to gain insight on how God reacts and responds when people go against His will and interfere with His chosen land and people. God has given explicit instructions that these things are not to be trifled with. What can we expect for the price of interfering with God's chosen land?

To understand that question, we must examine how God has dealt with those who would divide up and partition His land in the recent past, so that we may gain insight into what is going to happen in the future. This glimpse into the reactions of God will give us understanding where there may have been no understanding before. We need to search and learn from what has happened. Only then will we begin to see what God has in mind for the future.

Chapter Four

THE CONSEQUENCES OF INTERFERENCE
IN ISRAEL

Let's take a look at the approach the world has chosen to attain peace in the Middle East. The world has been demanding "land for peace," a doctrine insisting that Israel give back portions of the land they have gained in the wars fought in the past. This land is rightfully theirs by a decree from God, a fact that is ignored by those who want to broker peace deals in this area. Land-for-peace has never worked, and frequently the land that has been given back has become the launch pad for attacks against the state of Israel.

Let's be clear about what the Lord has said. God has given Israel the land east of the Nile River to the land west of the Euphrates River. It's not up to man to give his approval for what God has decreed. When the nations of the world interfere and try to override the Lord, and take away land that the Lord says belongs to Israel, they are going against God. That places whoever does this in a very precarious position. They are in essence fighting against God, a stance no Christian or rational person should ever take.

The Lord has not only been clear about the land that he wanted to give to Israel, but He has unequivocally stated that Israel is not to give any of this land away. God was absolutely clear when He commanded Israel not to part with the land that He had granted them. "And they shall not sell of it, neither exchange, nor alienate the firstfruits of the land; for it is holy unto the Lord." (Ezekiel 48:14)

God has also commanded the Jewish people not to make any peace deals concerning the land that He has granted them. He knew that peace deals would lead to Israel losing control of their land and straying from Him. So God strictly forbade Israel from entering into peace deals and letting others live in their land. "Thou shalt make no covenant with them, nor with their gods. They shall not dwell in thy land, lest they make thee sin against me: for if thou serve their gods, it will surely be a snare unto thee." (Exodus 23:32, 33)

The land-for-peace deals are an unmitigated disaster for Israel and can also have repercussions for the nations that insist on these deals. A case in point is the area known as the Gaza strip. Israel had captured the Gaza strip in the Six Day War of 1967. It is part of the area that God has said belongs to Israel. The United States, when trying to promote peace in the region of the Middle East, insisted that Israel give the Gaza strip to the Palestinian people in 2005. Israel finally gave in to the demands of President George W. Bush and the United States and gave back the Gaza strip in 2005. They forfeited their land even though thousands of Israeli citizens had built homes and businesses in that area. There were 9,000 Israeli settlers and twenty five communities affected by the forced withdrawal from the Gaza area.[3] The Jewish people, many weeping and crying for their rightful property, were driven from

---

3   William Koenig, *Eye to Eye* (Alexandria, VA: About Him Publishing, 2006), p.161.

the Gaza strip by their own army at the insistence of the United States. The notice for eviction was given on August 15th, 2005, and by August 23rd all Israeli citizens had been forcibly removed and the demolition of their homes was started to prevent them from returning to the area.

My country, the United States, regardless of our good intentions, had directly countermanded a decree from God and interfered with God's plan for this area. Did the United States face repercussions from this unwise act? I'll let you decide: on the very day the last of the Israeli settlers left the Gaza strip, August 23rd, a tropical depression formed near the Bahamas and on August 25th was upgraded to a hurricane. This hurricane was known as Katrina, and on August 29th this monstrous beast of a storm pummeled the states of Louisiana, Mississippi and Alabama and caused untold devastation to the city of New Orleans. When Hurricane Katrina slammed into the affected areas and New Orleans on August 29th, 2005, almost one million citizens of the United States were crying and weeping as they left their homes, much like the Israeli citizens withdrawing from the Gaza strip.[4] Hurricane Katrina left untold death and devastation in its wake, and catastrophic damage that in many cases has still not been repaired to this day.

Is this the only time that the United States has faced consequences for interfering with Israel and insisting that she give up land for peace? No, it is not. In his book, *Eye to Eye, Facing the Consequences of Dividing Israel*, William Koenig points out the consequences the United States has faced because of our insistence on parceling up the land or insisting on a Palestinian state in land that God has said belongs solely to the nation of Israel. The list

---

4   William Koenig, pp. 39-41, 49, 113, 154, 177.

is profound and shocking, and stretches from Presidents George H.W. Bush, Bill Clinton, George W. Bush, and President Obama.

For example, on October 18th, 1991, the United States announced the planned Madrid Peace Conference where our country led the call for the nation of Israel to start giving up portions of their land in order to obtain peace. On October 20th, 1991, the Oakland Firestorm started and became the greatest conflagration our nation had seen in this century with thousands of homes destroyed and catastrophic loss of life.

The Madrid peace conference began on October 30th, 1991, with US and world leaders insisting that the nation of Israel be divided. The same day, October 30th, 1991, the perfect storm formed over the eastern portion of the United States and became the worst storm to hit the United States in over 100 years. President George H.W. Bush's home was damaged in Maine.

After agreeing to meet again, the Madrid peace conference reconvened on August 24th, 1992. The United States led the call for Israel to give up land for peace, and on the same day, August 24th, 1992, Hurricane Andrew, an almost unheard of category five hurricane with sustained winds of 177 miles per hour, struck southern Florida and demolished everything in its path. Up to that date in time, Hurricane Andrew was the worst natural disaster in the history of the United States, only to be surpassed by Hurricane Katrina in 2005.

President Bill Clinton met with Syrian President Haffez Assad on January 16th, 1994, and called on the nation of Israel to leave the Golan Heights, another area that the Lord had said belongs to Israel. The next day on January 17th, 1994, a massive earthquake struck Northridge, California and caused economic losses totaling 16.2 billion dollars.

On January 31st, 2003, Secretary Collin Powell announced that President Bush would be more involved in the push for a Palestinian state within the borders of Israel. The goal was to have a nation for Palestine by 2005. The next day, on February 1st, 2003, the Space Shuttle Columbia broke up upon re-entry over the state of Texas, President Bush's home state. Among the dead in this tragedy was an astronaut from Israel, Ilan Ramon. The vast majority of the debris fell in an area of Texas that is so astounding that it almost defies rational understanding. Significant portions of the debris fell on and around a city in Texas with a most unlikely name… Palestine, Texas.

Is it possible that all of these instances are just coincidence? The list goes on and on like this. Time and time again, by the insistence of many different Presidents, the United States has demanded that Israel give up some of her land for peace. The consequences of these demands have been consistent and unwavering. The United Stated has been inundated with natural disasters that start on the day or within twenty four hours that our lands-for-peace plans are announced. Are the consequences of our actions always limited to the effects of natural disasters on our nation?

What about the granddaddy of horrific events that have struck our country? I'm referring to the day that is seared into the memory of every American who was alive at the time. The day that will never be forgotten; the day when the United States was maliciously attacked and suffered catastrophic loses. That day was 9/11 in 2001. That day will always be remembered as our day of infamy, our day of loss, the day when America was stricken, the day when thousands of Americans lost their lives, the day of darkness, the day of incalculable harm, the day of mourning, the day of the worst terrorist attack in the history of our nation. No one who experienced it will ever forget that day on September 11th, 2001.

That day left a wound and scar that seared the very soul of what it is to be an American—a loss so terrible that the effects are still being felt to this time.

Could it be that the United States was again making a decision that called on Israel to give up a portion of their country just prior to the tragic events of 9/11? As unbelievable as this may sound, that is precisely what happened. President George W. Bush was trying to reassure the nation of Saudi Arabia that Israel would not have a more favorable status in the peace negotiations than other Arab nations. George W. Bush was just putting the finishing touches on a speech, where for the first time, a US President was going to call for a Palestinian state inside the boundaries of modern-day Israel. The speech was for all intents and purposes finished on September 10th, 2001. The next day, everything changed when our nation was attacked. As the events of 9/11 unfolded, it became clear that nothing would ever be the same again. The President who had been so willing to appease different Arab nations, now found himself faced with a war on terror, and his presidency would never be the same again.

Look back on these events and our Presidents that have led the call for the division of Israel. It seems that each and every one of these men appeared to be honest and sincere in their efforts to attain peace in a region that has historically known no peace. They all had good intentions but their land-for-peace plans have always suffered a serious flaw. Their plans are contrary to what God has said He wants for this region. The Lord instructed that there should be no "land-for-peace" deals done with His land. And no one should be forming another country inside the boundaries that He has set for the nation of Israel. Everyone who ignores God's plan does so at their own peril.

What we need to realize is that this is one area where God will not compromise. The Lord has said what He has said, and it's not up to us to second-guess Him. God says what He means, and means what He says. All those that have disregarded what God has said concerning His land are suffering the consequences of their ignorance. The best of intentions will not shield us from the consequences of going against God and trying to countermand His directives. It is absolute foolishness to do so.

For most of us in this day and age, the Lord's stance on the land of Israel is somewhat surprising. We are used to seeing people do what is contrary to what God has told us to do, and then continue on with no immediate consequences for their actions. We have seen this so much that we are somewhat shocked when there is an immediate response to something God has told us we should not do. In fact, disregarding the Lord, and doing what we think should happen instead of following God's will has become so commonplace that we are surprised when God overrules our actions and places consequences on our failure to follow Him. We try to justify our actions and good intentions, never realizing that proceeding down that path may place us in direct opposition to God's will.

The Lord has the ability to see perfectly, we do not. Our vision is obscured by not being able to see the big picture, and our emotions and personal biases cloud our judgment and actions. In many cases, our best efforts just make the situation worse. Only God can make something good out of a hopeless situation. We need to trust Him.

The history of our responses to what God has said about His covenant land is an abysmal failure. We need to change course and consider what the Lord has said. God has granted to Israel a specific birthright—it is a land far larger than their present borders, and stretches from the land east of the Nile River to the land west of the Euphrates River. If we are really serious about "land-for-peace," then that area should define the borders of the nation of Israel. Anything less is going to lead to conflict. If any person or country proposes dividing up the land of Israel, or setting up another nation within God's prescribed boundaries for Israel…they will meet with immediate and absolute failure.

It is astounding that as history unfolds, we will not listen to what the Lord has said. Instead, we continue to promote peace in this area by insisting the Jewish people give away more and more of their land. This is a recipe for disaster, while heralded as the path to peace.

The consequences that the land-for-peace deals have had on the United States are remarkable. We have had the best of intentions for Israel, have never fought against them, and have never tried to actively destroy the Jewish people. Yet we have suffered some of the most devastating natural and man-made disasters to ever hit a country because of our efforts to divide Israel. Can we even contemplate what our fate would be if we tried to destroy the nation of Israel? Would there be any hope for our survival?

That is what we are going to discuss next—the fate of those trying to destroy the tiny nation of the Jewish people.

Chapter Five

THE OFFENCES OF ISRAEL'S NEIGHBORS

Many countries have actively tried to destroy Israel since it became a nation in 1948. Almost unrelenting violence started the day after they became a country, and continues on to this day. While the list of countries is numerous and diverse, some of the most egregious offenses have come from Israel's immediate neighbors.

Just exactly who are the neighbors of Israel? The following map highlights the countries surrounding the Jewish state.

As we study this map we notice the country of Lebanon to the immediate north of Israel. Syria and the area of the Golan Heights lie to the northeast of Israel. Directly east of Israel is the country of Jordan, and to the east of Syria and Jordan looms Iraq. Egypt borders Israel's western boundary.

What has been the history of these countries with their neighbor Israel?

All of these countries adamantly oppose Israel's existence and have been directly involved in attacks against the Jewish people.

Egypt, Syria and Iraq have all engaged in the three major wars against Israel since it became a nation. Jordan was involved in the Six Day War and the Yom Kippur War. Lebanon was involved in the fight against Israel right after it formed as a nation and incited hostilities again when it crossed into Israel on the July 12th, 2006 and ambushed two Israeli military vehicles. In that attack, three Jewish soldiers were killed and two were captured by Hezbollah. This prompted an Israeli response when the Israel Defensive Force (IDF) went into Lebanon to free the captured soldiers. A little over a month of fighting ensued before a cease fire agreement was enforced on August 14th, 2006.[5] To this day, the terrorist force, Hezbollah, in Lebanon, has consistently been involved in acts of aggression toward Israel. Hezbollah Chief Hassan Nasrallah has openly stated that he favors Jewish emigration to Israel because it makes killing all of the Jews easier when they are all gathered in one place.[6]

The situation in Syria is even worse. Syria was involved in all three of the major wars against Israel and has consistently taken advantage of opportunities to attack Israel. Syria is now embroiled

---

5   Ellen Knickmeyer, "2006 War Called a 'Failure' for Israel," *The Washington Post*, Jan. 31, 2008.
6   Charles Krauthammer, "Honor Auschwitz: Block Iran Bomb", *The Washington Post*, Jan. 31, 2015.

in an intense Civil War where forces loyal to the leader of Syria, Bashar al-Assad, are now battling the forces of the Islamic State of Iraq and Syria (ISIS), a group that formed from Al Qaeda in Iraq. The leader of ISIS is known as Abu Bakr al-Baghdadi, a self-proclaimed caliph or leader of all the Muslim people. The new leader of the caliphate, Abu Bakr al-Baghdadi is now consolidating his forces and leading attacks against the governments of Syria and Iraq. He has declared that when he is successful, the new leader of ISIS will focus all of his attention on the destruction of the nation of Israel.

Iraq is much like Syria but has become destabilized because of the withdrawal of US forces in the area. ISIS saw the pullout of US forces as an opportunity to take over a country that is already rabidly anti-Semitic. Iraq was involved in all three wars against Israel in the past, and fired SCUD missiles into Israel during the first Gulf War of 1991. The new leader of ISIS is taking advantage of every opportunity to destroy the government of Iraq and install himself as the new leader in this unstable area. When he does this, the new leader of the caliph will try to unite all of the countries of the Levant, the area predominately surrounding Israel and its neighbors, to turn their forces against Israel and annihilate all of the Jewish people. The new leader of the caliphate will not stop until he accomplishes this feat.

Jordan is another immediate neighbor of Israel. It lies to the east of the Dead Sea and has been involved in two of the major wars against the Jewish people. This area has a history of animosity toward Israel that has been unrelenting for almost 3,000 years.

Egypt is the nation that has led almost every attack on Israel in modern times. It was the instigator of two of the major wars against the Jewish nation and has spearheaded efforts to have the region of the Sinai returned to them. Most of the attacks against Israel in present times have occurred in the Sinai and Gaza strip areas. The Gaza Strip is the headquarters of the terrorist organization Hamas. The founding charter of Hamas calls not just for the annihilation of the state of Israel, but for the eradication of Jews everywhere.[7] Hamas has launched more rocket attacks against the Jewish people than all other nations combined. Almost the entire nation of Israel is susceptible to these attacks. The rocket attacks by Hamas are so numerous that they are almost incomprehensible. The following is a list of the attacks committed by Hamas from the Gaza strip, an area that the United States demanded be returned to the Palestinian people.

[8]

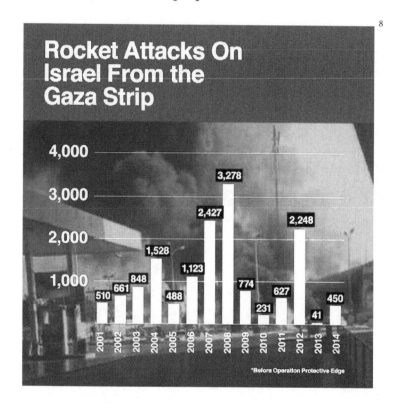

---

7   Ibid.
8   IDF Blog, "Rocket Attacks on Israel from Gaza", http://www.idfblog.com/facts-figures/rocket-attacks-toward-israel/.

As you can see, the number of rocket attacks against the Jewish people is astounding. It's hard to believe that Israel has tolerated the sheer number of attacks against them. Most countries would tolerate one or two attacks; Israel has endured 15,234 of these rocket attacks. In 2014, the Israeli Defense Forces (IDF) launched Operation Protective Edge and went into the Gaza strip on July 7th with the express purpose of eliminating the rockets and rocket launching capabilities of Hamas. The operation is ongoing and the rockets and their capabilities are listed below.

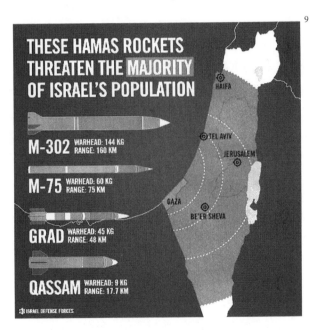

These rockets and their ranges present a serious threat to the security of the nation of Israel. No rational nation would tolerate this kind of threat to their citizens, and Israel has moved to eliminate all of the areas where these rockets have been hidden.

9   IDF Blog, "Rocket Attacks on Israel from Gaza", http://www.idfblog.com/facts-figures/rocket-attacks-toward-israel/.

To further complicate matters, ISIS has established a foothold in Egypt in the Sinai region, and is moving to strengthen their control of the area by threatening Jordan also. If ISIS gets into Jordan, it will completely encircle the nation of Israel and the new caliphate will control all of the neighbors surrounding the Jewish state. When this happens, Israel will have enemies on every side of them that will quickly move to eliminate God's chosen people. The fate of Israel looks grim indeed.

The only thing these countries have overlooked is the protective hand of God, and His response to all those who would threaten His people. The Lord will not stand idly by while these nations finalize their plans for the destruction of Israel. He will act and cause the plans of these nations to fail when they try to overthrow Israel, a nation and a land that God has set apart for Himself.

Chapter Six

THE FIRST WAR IN ISRAEL'S FUTURE, THE PSALM 83 WAR

The nation of Israel has experienced almost seventy years of continued attacks against it by those countries that are its immediate neighbors. That's practically an entire generation of attacks by those nations that are right next door to the Jewish people. God has given these countries ample time to stop their aggression against His chosen people, but instead they are ramping up their cries for the annihilation of the nation of Israel and entrenching themselves even more firmly in their hatred of the Jews. They are calling for Israel to be cut off as a nation and to be totally destroyed.

God's response to this is going to be totally unexpected by most people in the world today. His response will catch the nations of the world by surprise, and was written down almost three thousand years ago. The Lord has taken the words of Israel's neighbors from the headlines, and placed them in His Word and described their fate when they proceed on a path to destroy His people. He even lists the nations that will be involved by naming the people that reside within those countries.

How is it possible for God to do something like this? With the Lord, all things are possible. He sees the end from the beginning, and places these things in His Word with all the biblical patterns and precedents that go along with them. They are there for us to see if only we would study His Word and contemplate the things that He has written by the hands of His servants.

Where can we find what the Lord has decreed against Israel's neighbors who are fighting against her and trying to cut Israel off from being a nation? The answer lies with someone that most of us would not think of as a prophet. But he was a musician and a prophet in the royal courts of King David and wrote several of the Psalms. His name was Asaph and he wrote specifically about our day and time when he spoke of Israel in Psalm 83. The precision and insight with which he speaks could have been written yesterday instead of nearly three thousand years ago. Here is what he said concerning those who want to destroy Israel:

"Keep not thou silence, O God, hold not thy peace, and be not still, O God. For, lo, thine enemies make a tumult: and they that hate thee have lifted up the head. They have taken crafty counsel against thy people, and consulted against thy hidden ones. They have said, Come, and let us cut them off from being a nation; that the name of Israel may be no more in remembrance." (Psalm 83:1-4)

The common mantra of Israel's neighbors is that they have no right to exist and should be destroyed as a nation. Asaph notes this and then goes on and lists the countries that are saying these things. We will list the groups of people that Asaph names and then link them to their current counterpart countries.

The Nations of the Psalm 83 Coalition

"For they have consulted together with one consent: they are confederate against thee: The tabernacles of Edom, and the Ishmaelites, of Moab, and the Hagarenes; Gebal and Ammon, and Amalek; the Philistines with the inhabitants of Tyre; Assur also is joined with them: they have holpen the children of Lot. Selah." (Psalm 83:5-8)

Who are all of these people that are listed? Most of us are totally unfamiliar with these names because they are the names of groups of people in the Old Testament. Let's start at the beginning and break this down along with their present day location.

Edom is also known as Esau. (Genesis 36:1) Esau was the brother of Jacob who later was named Israel. Esau (Edom) ended up settling in the area south and to the east of the Dead Sea in an area known as Mount Seir. "Thus dwelt Esau in mount Seir: Esau is Edom." (Genesis 36:8) Mount Seir was a mountainous region between the Dead Sea and the Gulf of Aqabah, which is part of Jordan today. Edom has also been linked with the Palestinian people, and the Palestinian people have been acknowledged as the ancestors of Esau.

In Psalm 83 we saw that Edom is a major player in the confederation of nations that come against Israel. What is their fate? What are the consequences awaiting them? Their fate is spelled out in great detail in Ezekiel. "Son of man, set thy face against mount Seir, and prophesy against it, and say unto it, Thus saith the Lord God; Behold, O mount Seir, I am against thee, and I will stretch out mine hand against thee, and I will make thee most desolate. I will lay thy cities waste, and thou shalt be desolate, and thou shalt know that I am the Lord." (Ezekiel 35:2-4)

Remember that mount Seir is where Edom is located. There is no ambiguity in what God has said will happen to them. The Edomites are going to be destroyed, their cities are going to be laid waste, and their land will be desolate. This has not happened yet, but there is a very curious Scripture that may provide hints on a time frame when we can expect this to occur. In verse six it says, "Therefore, as I live, saith the Lord God, I will prepare thee unto blood, and blood shall pursue thee: since thou hast not hated blood, even blood shall pursue thee." (Ezekiel 35:6)

The word **"blood" is used four times in this Scripture. Could the use of blood occurring four times in this Scripture be a correlation to the four blood moons happening in 2014 and 2015?** If there is a correlation, then Edom and the country of Jordan where they reside, does not have much time left before a judgment will fall.

The Lord explains the reasons for Edom's destruction. "Because thou hast had a perpetual hatred, and hast shed the blood of the children of Israel by the force of the sword in the time of their calamity, in the time that their iniquity had an end." (Ezekiel 35:5) Edom has taken many opportunities to shed the blood of the Jewish people, and even mocked God and boasted against the Lord. "Thus with your mouth ye have boasted against me, and have multiplied your words against me: I have heard them." (Ezekiel 35:13) Therefore, the fate of Edom has been sealed. "And I will fill his mountains with his slain men: in thy hills, and in thy valleys, and in all thy rivers, shall they fall that are slain with the sword." (Ezekiel 35:8)

The fate of the first player in the coalition against Israel is tragic. What awaits the others? The Ishmaelites are named second. Ishmael was the son of Abraham born to Hagar and was not the son of promise. Isaac was the son of promise. Through Isaac, God established His covenant. (Genesis 17:19) Ishmael was said to be a "wild man, his hand will be against every man." (Genesis 16:12) He would become the father of the Arab nations and eventually settled in the Arabian Peninsula to the south and east of Israel. Today this land is known as Saudi Arabia. There is a particular city in northern Saudi Arabia that is known as Dedan. Dedan is mentioned specifically in the Scriptures in connection with the destruction of Edom.

"Therefore, thus saith the Lord God; I will also stretch out mine hand upon Edom [Jordan], and will cut off man and beast from it; and I will make it desolate from Teman; and they of Dedan [Saudi Arabia] shall fall by the sword." (Ezekiel 25:13)

When the land of Jordan is being destroyed, portions of the land of Saudi Arabia, specifically Dedan, which is in northern Saudi Arabia, will also fall by the sword. The Lord specifies the means by which He will carry out their destruction.

"And I will lay my vengeance upon Edom *by the hand of my people Israel*: and they shall do in Edom according to mine anger and according to my fury; and they shall know my vengeance, saith the Lord God." (Ezekiel 25:14) (Italics mine)

Here we are given the information on how God is going to destroy the nations of the coalition. He is going to accomplish this by the **"hand of my people Israel."** The Israeli Defense Force (IDF) is going to be the one carrying out this destruction. This is a key piece of information because it tells us the means by which God is going to defend the nation of Israel. It is **by the IDF that the destruction of the nations surrounding Israel is going to be accomplished**. Portions of Saudi Arabia will be included in this destruction.

We have examined two of the members of the coalition coming against Israel, and have learned some interesting facts. The destruction of these people will be carried out by the IDF, and there is a hint of four blood moons in the timing of the attack.

Moab is mentioned next in the list. Who was Moab? Moab was a son of Lot by his eldest daughter. (Genesis 19:37) The people of Moab also currently live in the country of Jordan, to the east of the Dead Sea. The nation of Jordan is going to be destroyed by the IDF, and Moab suffers the same fate as the rest of the nations. "And I will execute judgments upon Moab, and they shall know that I am the Lord." (Ezekiel 25:11) The destruction of Moab is going to be so severe that it will be like the destruction of Sodom and Gomorrah, and their destruction will open the way for the people of Israel to live where they live. We are given this insight in Zephaniah.

"Therefore as I live, saith the Lord of hosts, the God of Israel, surely Moab shall be as Sodom, and the children of Ammon as Gomorrah, even the breeding of nettles, and saltpits, and a perpetual desolation: the residue of my people shall spoil them, and the remnant of my people shall possess them." (Zephaniah 2: 9)

The Hagarenes are a part of the coalition of nations coming against Israel also. Who are the Hagarenes? They are ethnically the people of Hagar. Hagar was the mother of Ishmael, and a concubine of Abraham. She was the one given to Abraham by Sarah when Sarah couldn't conceive a child. Hagar was an Egyptian (Genesis 16:1), so the Hagarenes are the Egyptian people. The nation of Egypt has been the aggressor against Israel many different times and now is paying the price as Egypt has degenerated into a country at war with itself. This was foretold in God's word in Isaiah. "And I will set the Egyptians against the Egyptians: and they shall fight every one against his brother, and every one against his neighbor, city against city, and kingdom against kingdom." (Isaiah 19:2)

The Muslim Brotherhood has taken over Egypt, and now members of ISIS are in the country too—all vying for control of this war-torn nation. Regardless of which group eventually controls Egypt, it is clear that Egypt is bent on destroying Israel. When they attempt to do so, their fate has been foretold in Isaiah.

"In that day shall Egypt be like unto women: and it shall be afraid and fear because of the shaking of the hand of the Lord of hosts, which he shaketh over it. And the land of Judah shall be a terror unto Egypt, every one that maketh mention thereof shall be afraid in himself, because of the counsel of the Lord of hosts, which he hath determined against it." (Isaiah 19:16, 17)

Egypt will lose the conflict with Israel, and Israel will set up five cities in the land of Egypt, most likely in the area east of the Nile River, in the land that the Lord gave them. "In that day shall five cities in the land of Egypt speak the language of Canaan, and swear to the Lord of hosts; one shall be called, The city of destruction." (Isaiah 19: 18) The people in these cities will speak Hebrew and be loyal to the Lord. Even though the Lord will smite Egypt, and they will lose the war in the coalition of nations coming against Israel, the Lord will also eventually heal their nation and cause them to return to the Lord. "And the Lord shall smite Egypt: he shall smite and heal it: and they shall return even to the Lord, and he shall be entreated of them and shall heal them." (Isaiah 19:22)

The fate of the Egyptian people has been written in God's Word. Next on the list is Gebal, a place that seems totally unfamiliar. Gebal was a city on the coast of the Mediterranean Sea. It is in the present country of Lebanon in the northern parts of that nation. Lebanon is the home of the terrorist group Hezbollah and Hezbollah has been dedicated to the destruction of Israel since its inception in 1982. Lebanon is a country that has constantly been clashing with Israel through the leadership of Hezbollah, and is a country destined to share the fate of another city found within its borders.

Tyre is also on the list of Psalm 83, and is found in Southern Lebanon. Again, this is an area dominated by Hezbollah, a Shiite Islamic group. Tyre is a city that is mentioned specifically in the Bible and is a thriving trade center and the center for operations of Hezbollah. There is no question that Hezbollah has stated they favor the complete and total destruction of Israel, and their actions have shown this many times. Tyre's fate is described in Isaiah where it clearly states that Tyre is going to be laid waste. "The burden of Tyre, howl, ye ships of Tarshish; for it is laid waste, so that there is no house, no entering in: from the land of Chittim it is revealed to them." (Isaiah 23:1) The destruction of Tyre is going to be so complete that not even a house is going to be left standing. The fate of Tyre is similar to the fate and destruction of Egypt. "As at the report concerning Egypt, so shall they be sorely pained at the report of Tyre." (Isaiah 23:5) This is surely an area you do not want to be in when the time of their annihilation arrives.

Ammon is mentioned next on the list in Psalm 83 of the coalition of nations calling for Israel's destruction. Who was Ammon? Ammon was a son of Lot by his youngest daughter. (Genesis 19:37) The ancestors of Ammon settled in the northern parts of what is modern day Jordan. As we have already seen, the current nation of Jordan has a horrible fate awaiting her. The disposition of the Ammonites, the descendants of Ammon, will be no different. Some of their cities will become smoldering ruins as foretold by Jeremiah.

"Therefore, behold, the days come, saith the Lord, that I will cause an alarm of war to be heard in Rabbah of the Ammonites; and it shall be a desolate heap, and her daughters shall be burned with fire: then shall Israel be heir unto them that were his heirs, saith the Lord." (Jeremiah 49:2)

Many of the places of the people of Ammon will be destroyed by the IDF. When this happens, it appears that Saudi Arabia (Dedan) will move to help Ammon, but they are warned by God to turn back and dwell deep in their own country, or the Lord will allow the calamity reserved for Esau to fall on them also.

"Flee ye, turn back, dwell deep, O inhabitants of Dedan; [Saudi Arabia] for I will bring the calamity of Esau upon him, the time that I will visit him." (Jeremiah 49: 8)

If Saudi Arabia does not heed the warning, then it shall suffer destruction at the hands of the IDF also.

The people of Amalek, or the Amalekites are also mentioned next in Psalm 83. Who was Amalek? The Amalekites settled in the Negev desert south of the Dead Sea. The Amalekites first became enemies of Israel when they attacked the Israelites after crossing the Sea of Reeds when they were leaving Egypt. This places the Amalekites in what is today northeastern Egypt. From that time on there has been almost perpetual war between Israel and the descendants of Amalek.

The Lord has told Israel that when they are gathered to the land of their inheritance, that they are to "blot out the remembrance of Amalek from under heaven."

"Therefore it shall be, when the Lord thy God hath given thee rest from all thine enemies round about, in the land which the Lord thy God giveth thee for an inheritance to possess it, that thou shalt blot out the remembrance of Amalek from under heaven; thou shalt not forget it." (Deuteronomy 25:19)

Amalek will suffer the same fate that awaits the others that have fought against Israel and tried to destroy it.

Next on the list of Psalm 83 are the Philistines. The Philistines are the group that is now known as the Palestinians. This is an ethnic label to describe three different groups of Arab people. These three groups are the Palestinian refugees, the Palestinians of the West Bank, and the Palestinians that are located in the Gaza strip. These Palestinians are comprised of various groups mixed together, all of different origins, but many of them traceable to Esau, who was the father of the Edomites.[10]

There is no doubt that the Palestinians are more involved than any other group in the constant state of war that is waged against the Jewish people. This includes the over 15,000 rocket attacks from the Gaza strip by the Palestinian people led by Hamas, the group that wants to kill the Jewish people everywhere. On the West Bank, Israel had to erect a wall between themselves and the Palestinians because of the constant attacks.

No one group has done more to annihilate the Jewish people than the Palestinians, and because of this, the judgment against them is going to be very severe. The Palestinians are going to experience what they are trying to do to the Jewish people. They are going to be destroyed, along with their cities. "For Gaza shall be forsaken, and Ashkelon a desolation: they shall drive out Ashdod at the noon day, and Ekron shall be rooted up. Woe unto the inhabitants of the sea coast, the nation of the Cherethites! The word of the

---

10   Bill Salus, "Are We Living in the Last Days?" http://www.arewelivinginthelast-days.com/road/mewar.html.

Lord is against you; O Canaan, the land of the Philistines, I will even destroy thee, that there shall be no inhabitant." (Zephaniah 2:4, 5)

Why is this going to happen to the Palestinians? It is because they have had a perpetual hatred for Israel and have tried to kill the Jews at every opportunity. "Because thou hast had a perpetual hatred, and hast shed the blood of the children of Israel by the force of the sword…" (Ezekiel 35:5)

How is this going to happen? As we have already discussed, the destruction is going to take place by the Israeli Defense Force, "By the hand of my people Israel" (Ezekiel 25:14), and there is going to be nothing left of them as the Israelis sweep them from the land like a fire. The description is detailed in Obadiah where it states that Israel is going to be like a flame, and the house of Esau like stubble.

"And the house of Jacob shall be a fire, and the house of Joseph a flame, and the house of Esau for stubble, and they shall kindle in them, and devour them; and there shall not be any remaining of the house of Esau; for the Lord hath spoken it." (Obadiah 1:18)

The Philistines are going to be included with the house of Esau when this happens. "And they of the plain the Philistines." (Obadiah 1:19) No more will the Palestinians be able to wage war on Israel. Their acts of aggression will cease as a fire destroys the stubble in the field because the Lord has decreed it. The Palestinians who constantly strive to destroy the Jewish people will themselves be destroyed.

Last on the list of nations in Psalm 83 is Assur. Assur has helped the "children of Lot". Who is Assur and the children of Lot? Assur is the Assyrians, from a city by the same name in the heart of the Assyrian empire. The children of Lot are Moab and

Ammon, two of the groups of people that we have already discussed. If we are going to understand the Assyrians, and their role in the attempt to destroy Israel, then we have to look at the area the Assyrians controlled to understand this prophesy.

The heart of the former Assyrian empire consists of the modern day countries of Syria and Iraq, although their empire stretched from Egypt to the borders of Turkey. The center of modern day Syria is the capital city of Damascus. Damascus is the oldest, continually inhabited city on the face of the earth. It is also associated with some of the worst terrorist groups that the world has ever known. ISIS is the latest terrorist group that is dominating the Syrian landscape. What do we know about ISIS and why is this important?

ISIS (Islamic State of Iraq and Syria) is significant because it represents the resurrection of a beast. This beast is a force that wants to control the entire world, and will stop at nothing to accomplish that goal. The beast I am talking about will not honor life, will demand that every Islamic person follow it's commands without question, will mercilessly execute any that stand in opposition to it, and will move to control the world and every person in it.

This beast is represented by an institution that just recently came back into being. This is an institution that was declared dead on March 3rd, 1924, and then recently came back into being on June 29th, 2014. This is a beast that was, then was not, and somehow is in existence yet again in our time—hinting at parallels found in seventeenth chapter of the Book of Revelation. Curiously enough, this beast came back into being after the first blood moon of April 15th, 2014.

The beast I am referring to is the caliphate, the office that demands obedience from the entire Muslim world, the office that at one time orchestrated the movements of the every Islamic person. This is the office that will not tolerate any dissenting opinions, and moves to destroy all that oppose it. And right now, the forces of the caliphate are rampaging across the countries of Syria and Iraq. What enrages this caliph more than anything else is the claim that he is not a true caliph, but a counterfeit caliph, a self-appointed caliph that was not chosen by the Muslim world. The most disturbing thing of all is that there is no one this caliph will not kill to legitimize his claims of office.

The man from ISIS claiming to be caliph now is Abu Bakr al-Baghdadi. We will discuss him in depth later, but the relevant part now is the fact that he is leading the forces in Syria and Iraq. Soon he will move to consolidate control in the area surrounding Israel by coordinating some sort of attack against the Jewish people. When he does this, he is going to unleash the response of the Israeli Defense Force, and initiate the scenario described in Psalm 83.

What is going to happen to Syria and parts of Iraq when the counterfeit caliph does this? The capital city of Damascus is going to be utterly obliterated. There is going to be nothing left of it except a ruinous heap. We are told this is the Book of Isaiah.

"The burden of Damascus. Behold, Damascus is taken away from being a city, and it shall be a ruinous heap." (Isaiah 17:1)

We can speculate on how this will occur, but the most likely scenario is the use of limited nuclear weapons. Every expert agrees that Israel has nuclear weapons, and some of their arsenal includes nuclear weapons of limited size and capability. If Israel were to use one of these weapons to attack Damascus, then the result would be exactly what we read in Isaiah. Regardless of the means to accomplish it, Damascus is going to be annihilated and the Assyrians are going to be dealt a serious blow. The fate of the Assyrians is given in Zephaniah.

"And he will stretch out his hand against the north, and destroy Assyria, and will make Nineveh a desolation, and dry like a wilderness." (Zephaniah 2:13) Nineveh was the ancient capital of Assyria and is located across the Tigris River from Mosul in Iraq.

We have now described the fate of each and every nation and people described in the Psalm 83 coalition of nations that move for war against Israel. Their fates are devastating and catastrophic, and have been described in detail in God's Word.

It might be helpful to list the nations and peoples from Psalm 83 so we can keep them straight and see how they differ from other people that move against Israel in the future. Here is the list.

Nations and People of Psalm 83:

- Edom-Esau — located in Southern Jordan

- Ishmaelites — Saudi Arabians

- Moab — Central Jordanians

- Hagarenes — Egyptians

- Gebal — Northern Lebanon

- Ammon — Northern Jordanians

- Amalek — Arabians south of the Dead Sea and Northeastern Egypt

- Philistines — Palestinians of the Gaza strip and West Bank, with Hamas dominating them

- Tyre — Lebanon and Hezbollah terrorist group

- Assyria — Syrians and portions of Iraq with ISIS dominating them

- Children of Lot — Moab and Ammon

This is the list of coalition of nations that will move against Israel as described in the Psalm 83 war.

Chapter Seven

IMPORTANT POINTS FROM THE PSALM 83 WAR

We discussed many things about the fate of the people and countries that come against Israel in the Psalm 83 war. Perhaps it would be good to summarize some of the things we have learned while investigating their destiny. This will help to clarify our thinking and help us realize some of the salient things we can learn when reviewing this information.

Here are some of the important points:

- God has tolerated aggression against His chosen people Israel for almost a generation (70 years) since they became a nation in 1948.

- Asaph, a musician of King David and a prophet (2 Chronicles 29:30) wrote about the coalition coming against Israel in Psalm 83.

- The people listed in Psalm 83 war are distant relatives of Israel.

- The people and nations listed in the Psalm 83 war occupy land God gave to Israel. (Genesis 15:18)

- Imagery of blood moons is hinted at in the time frame of the Psalm 83 war. (Ezekiel 35:6)

- Reasons for the destruction of these nations is given. (Ezekiel 35:5)

- God is going to accomplish the destruction by the hand of his people (IDF) as described in Ezekiel. (Ezekiel 25:14)

- Moab will be destroyed like Sodom. (Zephaniah 2:9)

- Egypt will lose land in this war and five Israeli cities will be established in Egypt. (Isaiah 19:18)

- Tyre, closely associated with Hezbollah in Lebanon, will be destroyed. (Isaiah 23:1)

- The Ammonites will be destroyed. (Jeremiah 49:2)

- God warns the Saudi Arabians not to get involved or they will be destroyed like Edom. (Jeremiah 49:8)

- The Palestinians, who are controlled by Hamas, will be destroyed. (Zephaniah 2:4-5)

- There will be none remaining of the house of Esau. (Obadiah 1:18)

- The Syrian city of Damascus will become a ruinous heap. (Isaiah 17:1)

- Caliphate (beast) reestablished on June 29th, 2014 after the first blood moon of 2014.

- ISIS dominates Syria and Iraq (Assyria) and Assyria will be destroyed. (Zephaniah 2:13)

- The Israeli Defense Force (IDF) will accomplish this destruction, most likely, with the use of limited Nuclear Weapons. (Isaiah 17:1, Jeremiah 49:2, Obadiah 1:18, Isaiah 23:1)

While we have learned many important points about the fate of these nations, one of the most important things we can discuss is why these things are going to happen. The removal of these people and nations will pave the way for Israel to inherit the land that God has decreed is for them. Israel will move to possess these lands that will stretch from the Nile River, to the River Euphrates after the land is vacated in the Psalm 83 war. The destruction, the fate, and the people that are dispossessed from these lands are described in detail in Ezekiel, Jeremiah, Isaiah, Obadiah, and Psalms. However, there is one book in the Old Testament that seems to sum this war up in the greatest detail, and it also gives us a critical clue when this war happens. The book summarizing the events of the Psalm 83 war is found in Zephaniah, in the second chapter.

Here we find a critical timing clue that sets this war apart from the end time war of Armageddon. It says, "Before the day of the Lord's anger." (Zephaniah 2:2) This is crucial because the battle of Armageddon comes after the "day of the Lord," and this war, the Psalm 83 war comes before the day of the Lord has begun. Because of this fact, it must be a separate war, and a war preceding the battle of Armageddon. We will examine this point more closely, but for now, let's review more of the summary of the Psalm 83 war that is found is Zephaniah.

Besides the timing of this war, the area and people being destroyed are listed and summarized. All of these people can be found on the list of nations of Psalm 83. The Gaza strip, and the cities found in the Gaza strip, home of the Palestinians, will be forsaken and become desolation. "For Gaza shall be forsaken, and Ashkelon a desolation: they shall drive out Ashdod at the noon day, and Ekron shall be rooted up." (Zephaniah 2:2)

Next, Lebanon is described, the land of two cities on the sea coast (Tyre and Gebal). "Woe to the inhabitants of the sea coast…I will even destroy thee, that there shall be no inhabitant." (Zephaniah 2:5) They are going to be destroyed, with no one left in them.

The fate of Moab and Ammon, two more participants in the Psalm 83 war, whose ancestors live in Jordan, are given. "Therefore as I live, saith the Lord of hosts, the God of Israel, Surely Moab shall be as Sodom, and the children of Ammon as Gomorrah…" (Zephaniah 2:9) Sodom and Gomorrah were two places that were literally swept out of existence because of judgment from God.

The Assyrians, who once inhabited the area of Syria and Iraq, are also mentioned in Zephaniah and told they will be destroyed. "And he will stretch out his hand against the north, and destroy Assyria; and will make Nineveh a desolation, and dry like a wilderness." (Zephaniah 2:13) This area is now infested by ISIS, a group so barbaric and cruel that the world will rejoice when they are destroyed.

All of these areas and people are listed in Psalm 83, and all are living on land that God said belongs to Israel. The removal of these people will pave the way for Israel to regain her rightful land. This idea is expressed in Zephaniah also. The coast is going to be for the house of Judah, and the remnant will be for all of Israel to possess. "And the coast shall be for the remnant of the house of Judah; they shall feed thereupon: in the houses of Ashkelon shall they lie down in the evening: for the Lord their God shall visit the, and turn away their captivity." (Zephaniah 2:7) "...the residue of my people shall spoil them, and the remnant of my people shall possess them." (Zephaniah 2:9)

Israel will have new borders

As a natural result of the Psalm 83 war, the area that Israel inhabits will increase dramatically. Israel will no longer be the tiny nation in the Middle East, but will emerge as a new powerhouse stretching from the Nile River in Egypt, encompassing the land of Jordan, the Gaza Strip, Lebanon, Syria, and parts of Iraq and Saudi Arabia.

Here is the new area that Israel will control:

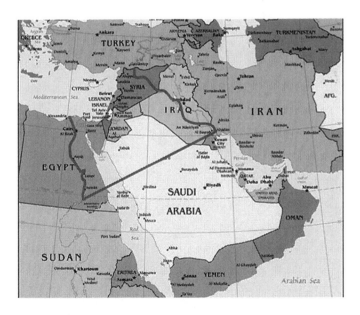

As you can see, it is quite large and will make Israel a new superpower in the area of the Middle East. This is the exact area that was designated for Israel by the Lord in Genesis. The malicious neighbors that were always attacking Israel and calling for their destruction will be vanquished.

While we have discussed the countries surrounding Israel, their acts of aggression, and the fate awaiting them, we have not discussed the biblical precedent or pattern for the Psalm 83 war, the most likely scenario that will trigger it, and when we can expect it to happen. That will be our next topic of discussion.

Chapter Eight

THE TRIGGER EVENT

In the first part of this book, we established a biblical pattern when we looked at the way the nation of Israel was broken apart in ancient times. It was not the result of one war, but a series of three wars that led to Israel's demise as a nation. The first of these wars was when the Assyrians led by Shalmaneser and later Sargon came against the Northern Kingdom of Israel (Samaria) and captured the ten tribes and led them off to the lands of the Assyrians.

We have just discussed the Psalm 83 war, and the destruction of the nations inhabiting the land given to Israel. What we have not yet discussed is the fact that the nations detailed in the Psalm 83 war were countries that inhabited the land given to the ten tribes of Israel (Samaria). The ten tribes (Samaria) were spread throughout the land occupied by present day Lebanon, the Golan Heights, Syria, Jordan and areas of Egypt.

Why do I bring up this point? Because in the first war that led to the destruction of their nation in ancient times, Israel lost the land that the ten tribes occupied. Now, after Israel has been reestablished in the land, the first of the end-time wars to fulfill Israel's prophetic destiny, the Psalm 83 war, is going to be a war where Israel reclaims the land of the ten tribes. In the ancient war, they lost the land of the ten tribes—in the Psalm 83 war they will regain that land.

This is the biblical pattern. In the ancient war Israel lost the land occupied by the ten tribes, in the future war in the end times, they will regain Samaria and the ten tribes. The Psalm 83 war accomplishes this pattern precisely. The area being regained, Samaria and the ten tribes, is exactly the same—in one Israel lost the area, in the other Israel will regain the area that had been lost.

The Biblical precedent is set. The ten tribes of Israel are set to once again become a part of a nation that lost them long ago.

The Trigger Event

Do we have any idea what causes the Psalm 83 war to start? In the ancient war, it was the Assyrians attacking the northern kingdom of the ten tribes. Curiously enough, the ancestors of the Assyrians are still in the countries of Syria and Iraq. Could it be that the Psalm 83 war is initiated by descendants of the Assyrians much like the ancient war?

Not only is it probable that this could happen, it is the most likely scenario. Remember that Syria and Iraq are controlled by ISIS. ISIS seems to hate everyone, even other Muslims who do not agree with them; but their greatest hatred is reserved for Israel. They will put aside their differences with other Islamic countries to launch an attack on the Jewish people. The common thread that unites them is their Islamic faith, even though there are theological differences between the Sunni and Shia branches of Islam.

The leader of ISIS, Abu Bakr al-Baghdadi, has a tremendous advantage working for him. All of Israel's immediate neighbors are Islamic and hate Israel, and may be willing to unite with him to accomplish their common goal of destroying the Jews. The leader of ISIS has assumed the role of caliph, and has declared that all Islamic people must follow his direction and orders. Even though self-appointed, he claims to speak for all Muslims. If he declares that all Islamic countries surrounding Israel must attack, it will place a compelling burden on all Islamic believers to follow the caliph. If they don't attack when commanded by the caliph, then they risk being destroyed by other Islamic nations. Even though they might not think that attacking Israel at the time is the proper course of action, most will probably agree to do so.

All of Israel's immediate neighbors have tried to destroy the Jewish state in times past. They probably won't need much convincing to try it again, especially with the promise of such a united force. These countries are filled with terrorist groups that have already stated that the destruction of Israel is their purpose in life. Hezbollah wants all the Jews in one place, so they will be easier to kill. Hamas' founding charter calls for the killing of Jews everywhere and the eradication of Israel. All of them are in agreement that they want to kill the Jewish people.

A coordinated attack, called for by the new caliph, is certainly within the realm of possibility. If this attack happens and the caliph uses any atomic, biological or chemical weapons, then the attacking nations can expect a swift and predetermined response from Israel. The worst kept secret in the Middle East is that if Israel is attacked and threatened with complete and total annihilation, it will exercise the Samson Option.

What is the Samson Option? The name is based on the biblical character Samson, who when faced with certain death at the hands of the Philistines who were holding him captive, chose to use his tremendous strength to bring down the temple of Dagon by pushing down the pillars holding the temple up. The result was the death of thousands of his enemies even though he himself was killed. The Samson Option that Israel has developed involves the use of nuclear weapons in its possession. When Israel is threatened by overwhelming military force, to the point where the continued existence of the nation is in doubt, it reserves the right to use nuclear weapons to defend itself.

Experts estimate that Israel has between 70 to 200 nuclear weapons in its possession.[11] The capabilities of their arsenal are as varied as the arsenal itself. While they have nuclear weapons capable of destroying huge swaths of land in the multiple kiloton variety, they most likely have weapons of limited nuclear capacity as well. These limited weapons will restrict the size and scope of the damage done. This includes suitcase sized nuclear devices and neutron bombs, which can be launched by aircraft or rockets. Neutron bombs kill by using enhanced radiation, but do little damage to the surrounding infrastructure. These would permit surgical strikes against an enemy bent on the destruction of Israel.

When we look at the prophetic descriptions of the damage to different areas of these nations recorded in the Bible, the descriptions certainly resemble the destruction we would expect from nuclear weapons. For example, Damascus is going to be *a ruinous heap.* (Isaiah 17:1) This is precisely what we would expect if nuclear weapons are used. Here is another example: the house of Jacob (Israel) is *going to set the house of Esau on fire,* and they will be like stubble and will be consumed. There will be no survivors of Esau. (Obadiah 1:18) There are more examples still: the area from Teman to Dedan (Jordan to Saudi Arabia) will *be laid waste.*

11   Robert S Norris, et al, "Israel Nuclear Forces, 2002", Bulletin of the Atomic Scientists, September-October 2002, (excerpt) 58 (5): 73-5, doI10.2968/058005020.

(Ezekiel 25:13) Moab (Jordan) will be *laid waste and brought to silence.* (Isaiah 15:1) Tyre (Lebanon) will be *laid waste so that there is no house left.* (Isaiah 23:1) The land of the Philistines (Palestine) *shall be destroyed so that there is no inhabitant left.* (Zephaniah 2:5)

Time and time again, the descriptions of the destruction of the nations in the Psalm 83 coalition are devastating. Will nuclear weapons be involved? Only the Lord knows for sure, but from the images provided about the fate of these nations, it certainly sounds like Israel is going to exercise the Samson Option and use nuclear weapons.

Here is a summary that may imply that nuclear weapons are going to be used by Israel:

- Damascus is going to be a ruinous heap (Isaiah 17:1)

- House of Esau set on fire and burned like stubble until they are consumed (Obadiah 1:18)

- The area from Teman to Dedan (Jordan to Saudi Arabia) will be laid waste (Ezekiel 25:13)

- Moab (Jordan) will be laid waste and brought to silence (Isaiah 15:1)

- Tyre (Lebanon) will be laid waste so that there is no house left (Isaiah 23:1)

- Land of the Philistines (Palestine) will be destroyed so that no inhabitants are left (Zephaniah 2:5)

The list of people and nations above are all contained in the coalition of nations described by Asaph in Psalm 83. Since we see from the list above that they are all going to be destroyed, the question becomes: What could possibly provoke such a response from Israel? How is the attack going to play out?

While there is no way to tell for sure until these things actually happen, we can speculate and hazard a guess as to what will lead to the Psalm 83 confrontation. While doing this, I must acknowledge that I am not a prophet, and have no special inside knowledge. But I do have God's Word that allows me to make certain deductions from the facts given. Knowing the players on the scene in the Middle East, I think it is safe to conclude the following from the facts we have, and postulate a scenario that will lead to the Psalm 83 confrontation.

The Psalm 83 War Scenario

Imagine this possible scenario with me: ISIS, under the leadership of Abu Bakr al-Baghdadi, the counterfeit caliph, moves to consolidate his leadership over the Levant (the area of Israel and its surrounding neighbors) by expanding aggressively in Syria, Iraq, Egypt and the areas surrounding Israel. In order to gain the prestige he feels he is due; Abu Bakr al-Baghdadi sets in motion a plan to attack Israel. If he can destroy Israel, then he thinks the prestige of destroying the enemy of all of Islam will catapult him into the position of a legitimate caliph—one who demands respect and obedience by all Sunni Muslims. A date is set when the counterfeit caliph demands that all of his forces, and the forces of the other countries surrounding Israel, launch their attack. At this point in time, Abu Bakr al-Baghdadi may even have access to atomic, biological, or chemical weapons. The time set for the attack comes, and the forces of ISIS move to destroy all of Israel.

When ISIS begins their attack, the Palestinian people under the control of Hamas in the Gaza strip use this opportunity to launch all of the rockets they have in their possession against Israel. Rockets rain down on all areas of Israel. The Palestinians celebrate as numerous areas in Israel are struck.

Hezbollah in Lebanon seizes the chance to strike at the Jewish people by launching an all-out attack against Israel. Nothing is held back as they prepare to strike deep into the heart of the Jewish nation.

Jordan immediately sees an opportunity to completely annihilate Israel as they have tried in the previous wars against Israel. They mobilize their army and prepare to cross into Israel to permanently end their war with the Jewish people.

Egypt, buoyed by the fact that they now have American made weapons, feel that they are invincible and set their army on the course to collide with the IDF. They prepare to cross into Israel and drive a dagger deep into the heart of the endangered nation. They feel nothing can stop them this time and move to complete what they have tried to do many times in the past.

The stage is set. Each component moves to accomplish their stated goal: the complete and total annihilation of the nation of Israel. By the end of this war, these combined forces will hope to achieve what no one has accomplished in modern times: the destruction of the nation of Israel.

Israel is attacked on all sides by huge armies bent on their destruction. ISIS is striking from the direction of Damascus, Hezbollah is on the rampage to destroy them from Lebanon, Hamas is raining rockets down on them from the Gaza Strip, Jordan is crossing into their territory from the direction of the Dead Sea, and Egypt is swarming up toward them into the southern part of their nation. Saudi Arabia is sitting on the sidelines, unsure of what to do. Israel is facing impossible odds and is being attacked on all sides by every neighboring country. They cannot ward off the attacks of all of their neighbors coming against them at once. Their plight is dire, the situation is hopeless. It is now time for desperate measures.

God's Response

What none of the players seem to realize is that God saw all of this happening almost 3,000 years ago. He saw it, and directed Asaph to write about it in the book of the Psalms. He provided details about the attacking coalition, the words they would say, and the fate awaiting them. God's Word also contains other tangible clues about the destiny awaiting those that do not listen to Him and who dismiss love for others and replace it with efforts to destroy God's people. God promised the Jews that once they returned to their land, He would watch over them. He will turn His face toward them once again in the form of a *Transcendent Event*. He will be their God, and they will be His people once again.

God's attention has been focused on the church for almost two thousand years. At some point in the near future, God will turn His attention back to His covenant people Israel, the people of His promises. At that point in time, God is going to respond to those attacking Israel by enforcing a law that He has implemented in the past to deal with those who would destroy His people. It is best described as the Law of Immediate Recompense.

The Law of Immediate Recompense

What is the Law of Immediate Recompense? First of all, what is recompense? According to *Webster's Dictionary*, recompense is something given or done in return for something else. Immediate means without delay. So by definition of these terms, the Law of Immediate Recompense means that whatever evil action you intend on someone else will be turned back upon you without delay. There is a scriptural reference that describes this law. In Jeremiah, we find God saying the following: "Recompense her according to her work; according to all that she hath done, do unto her." (Jeremiah 50:29) It says essentially the same thing in Ezekiel, "And I will judge thee according to thy ways, and will recompense thee for all thine abominations." (Ezekiel 7:8) The Law of Immediate Recompense means that God will turn the coalition's own evil intentions for Israel back on them without delay.

To understand the Law of Immediate Recompense we need to examine an area where it has been used in the past. That time is described in the Book of Esther. Esther was a beautiful Jewish maiden that was enthroned as a Queen to King Ahasuerus. The king did not know that Esther was Jewish. After she became Queen, a man arose to power who was second only to the King. His name was Haman and he was an enemy to the Jewish people. Haman's hatred of the Jewish people became more entrenched over time until it was so great that he plotted to kill all of the Jews.

By pretense and manipulation, Haman was able to get the King to endorse a decree that all the Jewish people of the land should be killed on a certain day. No Jewish person was to be spared; every man, woman and child was to be killed. Every Jew was supposed to die on that appointed day.

Queen Esther was made aware of the plot to destroy her people and intervened. At the peril of her own life, she asked the King to spare her and the lives of her people, the Jews. The King was incensed that he had been tricked and that Queen Esther's life was in danger. He demanded to know who had done this, and Queen Esther told him that it was Haman. The King decreed that Haman should be put to death on the very gallows he had constructed to kill Mordecai, Esther's uncle. Not only was Haman executed, but all of his sons and others who wanted to destroy the Jews. The king also decreed that on the appointed day of destruction, the Jews could defend themselves.

This is the Law of Immediate Recompense in action: Whenever someone seeks to kill or harm another person, their intentions are returned on them and they will have done to them what they intended for others.

Haman's evil intentions to kill all the Jews were turned back upon him, and he was executed upon the very gallows he had constructed for others.

The coalition of nations and people in Psalm 83 want the Jewish people to die. Because of this and the fact that they are going to attack the Jewish people, they will suffer the fate that they intended for Israel. They will be destroyed, condemned by their own words and actions. This is the Law of Immediate Recompense.

Israel's response to the Attack

When attacked from all sides like this, Israel will feel that they have no choice. They must act decisively or be completely destroyed. Therefore, Israel will use the Samson Option. They will see that the only way to stop the attacks on all fronts will be to use their nuclear arsenal. Israel will act, and they will release nuclear weapons on those nations who are attacking them.

The nations attacking Israel will have the Law of Immediate Recompense returned upon their own heads. They intend to destroy Israel, but they will be destroyed instead.

This is truly a sad time, and a time that didn't have to end this way, but actions have consequences, and Israel's neighbors will suffer the consequences of their actions.

Do we have any clues as to when this will occur? Will there be any signs given that will tip us off that these things are about to happen?

I believe that there are clues and signs, and all we have to do is to pay attention to them. One clue was alluded to in Ezekiel 35:6 where the word blood was used four times in a Scripture describing the fate of the Edomites, the first people on the list of nations in Psalm 83. Could this be a clue pointing us to the four blood moons? The sign that the Psalm 83 war will be happening in the near future will be written in the night sky with the completion of the Blood Moon tetrad.

The Blood Moon Sign

We have already discussed the sign of the Blood Moon tetrad. (Four Blood Moons back to back) If you remember, the Blood Moon tetrad formed after Israel became a nation in May of 1948. The Blood Moon tetrad manifested in 1949 and 1950, about a year later. During that time, Israel fought a war and gained land that would become the core of their nation.

The second Blood Moon tetrad happened in 1967 and 1968. The Six Day War happened in June of 1967, during the time of the tetrad. Israel was fighting a war and gaining more of the land it had been promised during this time also.

There has not been another Blood Moon tetrad until now in 2014 and 2015. The last Blood Moon will happen on September 28th, of 2015. In the two previous tetrads, Israel had been at war and ended up gaining a significant amount of land. If this pattern holds true in the future, then at some point in time after the manifestation of the Blood Moons of 2014 and 2015, the people of Israel are going to be embroiled in the fight of their life as the Psalm 83 war scenario engulfs them.

Why do I say "after" the manifestation of the tetrad? I say that because when carefully examine the pattern of the last two Blood Moon tetrads, we find a curious phenomenon. In the Israeli War of Independence tetrad, Israel formed as a nation in May 1948. The tetrad appeared almost a year later beginning in 1949. So first we had the war, and then the tetrad, not at the same time, but almost a year later. In the second tetrad, the tetrad manifested at the same time the war was being fought. The tetrad manifested beginning in 1967, and the war was fought in 1967; so we had the event and the tetrad at the same time.

In the final Blood Moon tetrad, the last one for hundreds of years, the final Blood Moon will be on September 28th, 2015. If the pattern is followed closely, then the tetrad will form, finishing in September of 2015, and then the war will occur, up to a year later. This inference is based on the fact that the Blood Moon sign is progressing in the following pattern: War-then Blood Moon, War and Blood Moon at the same time, Blood Moon-then war. Based on this pattern, the Psalm 83 war could occur at any time within a year following the final Blood Moon of September 28th, 2015.

In all of the previous wars where the Blood Moon tetrad sign was given, Israel gained a significant amount of land. The Psalm 83 war will be no different. After Israel has vanquished the coalition of nations described in Psalm 83, it will for the first time in history, control the land that the Lord has set aside for Israel. This will be both a blessing and a tremendous burden. Israel will be in the land ordained by God for their nation, but the world will react as if the Jewish people had no right to defend themselves from the aggression of their neighbors and will raise a uproar against them. Israel will be denounced for their actions, and the world will rage, with anti-Semitism reaching new heights. The stage is being set for the second part of the *Transcendent Event*.

Chapter Nine

ISRAEL'S NEW REALITY

At the conclusion of the Psalm 83 war, Israel will emerge as a new superpower in the Middle East. It will move to possess the lands formerly occupied by Lebanon, Syria, Jordan and parts of Iraq, Saudi Arabia and Egypt. Its borders will stretch from the Nile River in Egypt to the Euphrates River in Iraq. On its northern border will be the nation of Turkey. Iran and the remnants of Iraq will loom on its eastern border. Egypt, the Sudan and Libya will be to the west of Israel, and Saudi Arabia will be present in the south.

With the new territory will come new challenges, the greatest of these will be the world-wide rise of anti-Semitism because of what Israel did to survive. They will attain this new area by the use of their nuclear weapons, by the hands of the IDF as Ezekiel said they would do in Ezekiel 25:14, *"By the hand of my people Israel."*

The world's response to Israel's use of nuclear weapons will be off the charts. They will become apoplectic in their cries against the Jewish people. Summits and forums will be convened, the United Nations will meet, and Israel's enemies will gather to lead the cry in the condemnation of Israel. The Jewish nation will be bludgeoned by the Press and targeted by the international community for world-wide ridicule and scorn.

Because of this, anti-Semitism will raise its ugly head once again. It will now become popular to condemn the Jews everywhere. God foresaw this happening also and told us in His Word that the nations would fume against His people like the raging sea, and roar like mighty waters. "Oh, the raging of many nations, they rage like the raging sea! Oh, the uproar of the peoples, they roar like the roaring of great waters! Although the peoples roar like the roar of surging waters, when he rebukes them they flee far away, driven before the wind like chaff on the hills, like tumbleweed before a gale." (Isaiah 17:12-13 NIV) There will be uproar in the streets by the people who are condemning Israel's actions, but when God moves to rebuke them, they flee like tumbleweeds before a storm. The outrage against the Jews will rise to a fever pitch as a chorus of nations voice their condemnation against the actions taken. When God moves to protect His people, the detractors will scatter like chaff before the wind.

The Jews are going to be the target of all kinds of discrimination, both overt and subtle. It will be like the 1930's all over again. Jews living outside of Israel will be targeted and suffer all kinds of abuse at the hands of their countrymen, many with the blessings of government officials. In many countries, being Jewish will be tantamount to having a death sentence placed on your head. The rights and security of the Jewish people not dwelling in the Holy Land will vanish almost overnight. There will be new cries for a holocaust against the Jews, and many will move to implement that strategy. The Jews will have to band together in order to survive. The call will go out for the Jews to return home to the Promised Land, to help fill the vast area of new land. Many will heed that call and return to the land of Israel.

The pressure on the United Nations to do something about what Israel has done will build until the UN is forced to react. Given the track record of resolutions that have not been favorable toward Israel, it's not hard to guess what the United Nations is going to do. There will be universal condemnation of Israel for the use of nuclear weapons, and the UN will draft a resolution saying that Israel can never use nuclear weapons again. If they do so, the UN will sanction immediate and complete annihilation of Israel by the forces possessing nuclear weapons in the international community. This statement is conjecture on my part, but it is conjecture backed up with an unrelenting history of resolutions passed by the UN that threaten Israel's existence. The UN does not want Israel to have nuclear weapons, and the only way to make the situation in the Middle East fair is to remove the nuclear weapons option for Israel. Consequently, if Israel ever uses nuclear weapons again, they will be nuked into oblivion by other nuclear forces. This will be the UN's way of solving the Jewish problem.

Israel's most powerful deterrent, the Samson Option, will be effectively removed by the international community, leaving them vulnerable to attack by those bent on their destruction. Israel will no longer be able to defend itself by surgical nuclear strikes against vastly superior forces swarming against them. They will be outnumbered and placed at a tremendous disadvantage when other nations possessing a huge superiority in conventional forces are arrayed against them. Without a miracle, they don't stand a chance if a massive army were to mobilize and come against them.

The world's plan for peace places Israel in a situation where it will be impossible to defend itself and sets the stage for the second war of the *Transcendent Event*.

Chapter Ten

NEW NEIGHBORS, NEW REALITIES

Israel will emerge from the Psalm 83 war in a stronger position than they were in before. The nations constantly attacking Israel have been removed and the new borders God has given them are more easily defensible. But Israel now has two new worries: their new neighbors, and worldwide disapproval of their actions.

Israel will immediately face some new challenges as a result of their takeover of these lands. First, there is the matter of all the widows and orphans left by the recently concluded war. Many of the men in these countries will have died in the war. What happens to those left devastated by the war?

The Lord will have foreseen this and made provision for the widows and orphans. They will be treated with care and respect and incorporated into God's people. No longer will they live in an atmosphere of hatred and constant warfare against another people. God will care for them, heal their wounds, and place them in an environment where they are safe and protected. The Lord will watch over them and make them a part of His people. God tells us this in Jeremiah:

"Leave thy fatherless children, I will preserve them alive, and let thy widows trust in me." (Jeremiah 49:11)

God will provide for the fatherless and the widows within the boundaries of Israel. His people will care for them and they will be safe from the ravages of war.

The Return of the Ten Tribes

Another challenge that the expanded nation of Israel will have is the need to populate the new area within its borders. In ancient times the nation of Israel had split up into two groups, the ten tribes and the tribes of Judah and Benjamin. The Lord said in Ezekiel that he was going to heal the divide between the two groups and make them one nation again. The time when Israel regains the land of the ten tribes is the perfect time for the ten tribes to begin returning to the expanded Israel. God said he would bring them home to Israel in the following Scripture:

"And say unto them, Thus saith the Lord God; Behold, it will take the children of Israel from among the heathen, whither they be gone, and will gather them on every side, and bring them into their own land: And I will make them one nation in the land upon the mountains of Israel; and one king shall be king to them all: and they shall be no more two nations, neither shall they be divided into two kingdoms any more at all." (Ezekiel 37:21, 22)

The ten tribes are coming home to a nation that has regained their land. They will never be separated from their brothers again. Israel will be whole once more, and members from each of the twelve tribes will populate the land again. The process will begin in earnest at the conclusions of the Psalm 83 war and will continue until all are eventually returned to the land.

They will be joined by their Jewish brothers from other countries because of the repercussions of the Psalm 83 war. Anti-Semitism will be rampant throughout the world and the safest place for a Jewish person will be in Israel.

The New Neighbors

The nation of Israel with its new territory will have a whole new set of problems. Israel will have expanded its borders up against some new neighbors, and it won't be long until trouble begins anew. With the expansion of its territory and new boundaries, here are the nations that now will be bordering the nation of Israel.

To the north is the country of Turkey. To the east is Iran and what is left of Iraq and to the west are the neighbors of Egypt including Libya, Algeria, and Tunisia and to the south is Sudan and Ethiopia. Does the listing of these countries sound familiar? Is there anything that rings alarm bells with this particular list of nations?

There should be. This is the list of nations involved in the Gog/Magog coalition that comes against Israel in the time of the last days. These are the countries from which a massive army will arise with the intention of crushing and destroying the Jewish people. And now, these countries are the new neighbors of Israel with its expanded borders. What is worse is the fact that many in these countries hate the Jewish people even more than their previous neighbors, and they are far larger countries with massive armies that dwarf the size of the Israeli Defense Forces. The amount of damage they can do against the nation of Israel is almost incalculable. This is the threat facing Israel with their new neighbors, and this time it looks like the Jewish people are doomed if their new neighbors ever decide to come against them.

All it will take is a spark to ignite the flames of hatred against the Jewish people as Israel once again finds itself surrounded by those who want to destroy them.

The Gog and Magog Coalition

Let's take a closer look at the Gog and Magog coalition of nations to see what insights we can gain from the Bible. They are found in the book of Ezekiel:

"Son of man, set thy face against Gog, the land of Magog, the chief prince of Meshech and Tubal, and prophesy against him, and say, Thus saith the Lord God; Behold, I am against thee, O Gog, the chief prince of Meshech and Tubal: and I will turn thee back, and put hooks into thy jaws, and I will bring thee forth, and all thine army, horses and horsemen, all of them clothed with all sorts of armor, even a great company with bucklers and shields, all of them handling swords: Persia, Ethiopia, and Libya with them; all of them with shield and helmet: Gomer, and all his bands; the house of Togarmah of the north quarters, and all his bands: and many people with thee." (Ezekiel 38: 2-6)

Who is the mysterious Gog? And who are all of these other people? Where do they come from?

This passage can be very confusing because of references with which most of us are unfamiliar. Here we find the title Gog for the first time, and also a reference to the land of Magog. Also, Gog is a chief prince in two more unfamiliar places, Meshech and Tubal. If we are going to gain further understanding, then we need to determine where the mysterious locations known as Magog, Meshech and Tubal are located.

How do we accurately determine the location of these enigmatic places? It's always helpful to use the best biblical resources available to us. Using this as our guide, the following map from the *Moody Atlas of Bible Lands* can be of great assistance to us in our quest for answers. It's a map of ancient Turkey with some key locations on it.

As you can see from this map, Magog, Meshech and Tubal are all easily located in different areas of ancient Turkey. In fact, two more of the players in the Gog, Magog alliance can be found in Turkey also. Gomer and Togarmah are listed as two more players in this coalition, thereby placing five members of the attacking entities in the nation of Turkey. This makes Turkey the predominate aggressor in the attacking coalition. Gog is the leader of the attacking entities from the land of Magog which we can see is in ancient Turkey.

It's as if the Bible is highlighting the fact that the modern day nation of Turkey is the location where five of the major entities of the Gog/Magog coalition lead an attack against Israel. And who is Gog? Gog is their leader or "chief prince." In other words, Gog is the leader that provides the impetus for the upcoming attack on Israel, and Gog has ties to Turkey for his power base. His power and authority come from Turkey as his power base because he is their "chief prince" and spokesman.

The *Moody Atlas of Bible Lands* is not the only source that places Meshech, Tubal, Magog, Gomer and Togarmah firmly in ancient Turkey. Some of the most prestigious Bible reference books, such as the *Macmillan Bible Atlas*, and the *Oxford Bible Atlas* also place these five entities in Turkey.

The other participants in this attack are more easily identifiable. "Persia, Ethiopia, and Libya with them, all of them with shield and helmet." (Ezekiel 38:5)

Persia is the modern day nation of Iran, and Ethiopia is what the biblical translators called the ancient land of "Cush," which is immediately south of Egypt in the land that is presently called Sudan.[12] Sudan became the "Islamic Republic of Sudan" in 1989 and has become a hotbed of Islamic repression against Christianity and other religions since then. Libya is identified as "Phut" and is the area west of Egypt in the modern day nation of Libya and includes small areas of Algeria and Tunisia also.

One characteristic of all the areas and nations identified as aggressors in Ezekiel thirty-eight and thirty-nine is that they are all Islamic nations. Turkey, Iran, Sudan, Libya, Algeria and Tunisia are all Islamic nations. They are separate and diverse

---

12 Bill Salus, "Are We Living in the Last Days?" http://www.arewelivinginthelast-days.com/road/mewar.html.

Islamic cultures, with some being Sunni Muslims and others Shia Muslims, but they are all Islamic nations.

Here is the list of the aggressor nations in the Gog/Magog coalition.

Gog/Magog Coalition:

- Magog-Turkey
- Meshech-Turkey
- Tubal-Turkey
- Persia-Iran
- Ethiopia (Cush)-Sudan
- Libya (Put)-Libya, parts of Algeria and Tunisia
- Gomer-Turkey
- Togarmah-Turkey

As you can see from this list, these nations are distinctive and different from the nations in the coalition of Psalm 83. The thing that ties all of these nations together, in both Psalm 83 and the Gog/Magog coalition, is the fact that all of them are Islamic. The Muslim religion unites them and all have expressed deep animosity toward Israel. In the Psalm 83 war, we discussed the fact that a new entity had arisen on the scene, a beast who will try to control all, the office of the caliph.

The caliphate was highjacked by a pretender to the office, a man who anointed himself, a beast of a man named Abu-Bakr al-Baghdadi. Abu Bakr may have resurrected the beast, but he will not be allowed to continue. He will be destroyed along with all of the others of the Psalm 83 coalition when they move to attack

Israel. With his death, a power vacuum will be created paving the way for the next caliph.

The Islamic world will not make the same mistake they made the first time when ISIS leader Abu Bakr al-Baghdadi seized control of the caliphate. They will move to legitimize the office and move the office of the caliphate back to the country that controlled it for 500 years. It is a country that controlled world power for centuries and established Islamic dominance over vast portions of the world. It led an empire, and now it wants control of the office of the caliphate back, and it has the means to accomplish its will.

The country is Turkey, the former leader of the Ottoman Empire, and the country where the office of the caliphate resided for 500 years. Turkey will rise up to assume what they feel is rightfully theirs—the office of the caliphate—and leading the way to assume control and speak as one voice for all the Muslim world... is the man who would be Gog.

Chapter Eleven

THE MAN WHO WOULD BE GOG

To understand the man who will take over the office of the caliph, we need to review some history. First of all, what exactly is the caliph and where did this office come from?

Caliph comes from the word "Khalifa" which means "succession" and came about after Muhammad died. It was unclear who should take over after Muhammad's death and many in the Muslim world felt the very best leader should step forward and lead Islam. This man would be known as the "caliph," and this "caliph" was supported by the Sunni branch of Islam. There were others who thought only a direct descendent of Muhammad should lead Islam, and this leader would be known as the "Imam." This form of leadership was favored by the Shia branch of Islam. The caliphate describes the form of Islamic government led by a caliph.

While the two factions were vying for control of all of Islam, a man stepped forward to assume the role of leadership over the entire Muslim world. He assumed the role of the first "Khalifa" or successor to Muhammad and declared himself the first

"Caliph," resulting in the formation of the "Caliphate." He was known by the name Abu Bakr, and he ruled the Islamic kingdom from 632 to 661 AD.[13]

When Abu Bakr died (the first caliph), a civil war began in the Muslim world. Those in the Sunni branch of Islam thought the strongest leader should take the place of Abu Bakr, and continue the office of the caliphate. Those in the Shia (or Shiite) branch of Islam thought that only a direct descendent of Muhammad should have the authority to lead the Muslim world, and this man would be known as the "Imam." These two branches of Islam began fighting for control of Islam with the Sunnis placing another caliph in control, and the Shias placing the first Imam in control of their branch of Islam.

This power struggle led to huge divisions in the Islamic world, with the Sunni division controlling the caliphate emerging as the stronger of the two versions of Islam. The caliphs dominated by killing their rival Imams by subterfuge. The first eleven Imams were killed by poisoning and one was beheaded on the orders of the different caliphs.[14] The 12th and final Imam had to go into hiding in order to preserve his life. The twelfth Imam is said to have disappeared (gone into occultation) in 872 AD,[15] and those in the Shiite branch of Islam are anxiously awaiting his return. We will discuss more on this later because this is an important point in end times discussion.

Thus the caliphate emerged victorious in the conflict to seize control of the Islamic world. The caliphs dominated from 872 AD onward. The office of the caliphate is said to speak with one voice

---

13 Encyclopaedia Britannica, online version, "Caliphate, Islamic History," by the editors, last updated 10-28-2014.
14 Wikipedia, "Imamah (Shia doctrine)," http://en.wikipedia.org/wiki/Imamah_ (Shia_doctrine).
15 Ibid.

for all the Muslim people in the world, and it is the duty of all diligent Muslims to follow and carry out the orders of the caliph. There is to be no questioning or dissention in the ranks when instructions are given by the caliph. Those orders are to be followed implicitly and have been throughout the centuries.

The caliphate became an institution headquartered in Turkey with the conquest of Constantinople by the first Turkish caliph Mehmed II in 1453.[16] After him, the office of the caliphate remained in Turkey (Ottoman Empire) until it was abolished on March 3rd, 1924 by Mustafa Kemal, who later assumed the name Ataturk, and became the leader of Turkey. The last official caliph, Abdulmecid II, was deposed by Turkey's leader Mustafa Kemal Ataturk in 1924.[17]

The Islamic world considered the abolition of the caliphate to be an inconsolable loss. The entire Islamic world considered the action to be a loss of their voice, and consequently the Muslim community degenerated into different warring factions, constantly at odds with each other. There was no longer a single, united Islamic voice.

The New Leader

This is the scene upon which the man who would be Gog will emerge. The office of the caliphate was abolished on March 3rd, 1924. On June 29th, 2014, a pretender to the office of caliph re-emerged after it had been vacant for 90 years.

The man who will be known as Gog may have watched as the counterfeit caliph, Abu Bakr al-Baghdadi, declared himself as ruler

16   Selcuk Aksin Somel, *The A to Z of the Ottoman Empire*, (Lanham, MD: Scarecrow Press, 2003), p. 179.
17   Wikipedia, *"The Ottoman Caliphate,"* last revised 28 March, 2015, http://en.wikipedia.org/w/index.php?title_Ottoman_Caliphate&oldid=653919004.

over the Muslim world. Gog sees history repeating itself as the new leader assumed the name of Abu Bakr, the name of the first caliph who succeeded Muhammad. Gog knows that this is a stunt to lend credibility to a man who assumed the title himself, he was not chosen by the body of Islam. As with all pretenders, Gog knows that the counterfeit caliph will make a mistake, a mistake that will lead to his undoing. When he does this, Gog will be ready to step in and assume control in the ashes of the pretender's defeat.

While the Islamic world is still reeling from the defeat of Abu Bakr al-Baghdadi at the hands of the Israeli Defense Forces and they move to control all the land that the Lord gave to them, the seeds of victory have been planted for Gog. The defeat of Abu Bakr al-Baghdadi allows Muslims to move the office of the caliphate back to the land where Gog feels it rightfully belongs, the nation of Turkey. After all, Turkey controlled the office of the caliphate for 500 years, and it was in Turkey that it was disbanded. It only seems right that the office of the caliphate should be back in Turkey. And when the caliphate is reinstated there, Gog will become the new caliph.

Gog is waiting for the moment that he will emerge as the leader of the Caliphate. When that happens, he will be the legitimate leader of the body of Islam. Israel may have obtained a victory in defeating their Islamic neighbors surrounding them (The Psalm 83 War), but now they are more vulnerable than ever. Gog will make sure that Israel's nuclear capabilities are taken from them in the halls of the United Nations. Israel will be emasculated. Gog will cause an uproar among the nations as he equates Israel's defensive actions in the Psalm 83 war as crimes against humanity. His minions will lead the call for the punishment of the Jewish people, and Gog will be waiting in the background to make his next move.

When Gog emerges on the scene as the new caliph for the entire Muslim world, he will have a significant power base in the nation of Turkey. He will control the land of Magog in Turkey, as well as the areas where Meshech, Tubal, Gomer and Togarmah are located. Turkey was the power behind the Ottoman Empire, the empire that seized control after the collapse of the Roman Empire. The Ottoman Empire has all the characteristics of the seventh beast empire described in Revelation 17:10-11. The Ottoman Empire lasted until the end of World War I. Turkey, its surviving entity, still has formidable power in the Middle East, and is unmistakably a Muslim country. It has a huge standing army and has demonstrated the ability to use that army effectively many times.

As leader of the caliphate, Gog will use his authority to call for other nations to prepare for an assault against Israel. Other nations such as Iran will be obliged to follow his call. If they refuse the call of the caliph, they will be ostracized by other Islamic nations. For its own reasons, Iran will not refuse the call to prepare for war against Israel. Iran has been trying to incite war with Israel for many years. By their leader's own admission, the purpose of their nuclear weapons program is to develop a bomb to use against Israel. The Iranian leaders feel that if they use a nuclear weapon against Israel, then the chaos of war will force the 12th Imam to come out of hiding and rightfully lead the Islamic world.[18]

Iran is home to the Shia Islamic group that believes in the return of the 12th Imam. The 12th Imam is prophesied to return during a time of great tribulation for the Muslim world, when the forces of Islam have suffered a great defeat.[19] If Iran does not have a workable nuclear weapon when Gog calls for an attack on

---

18 "Iran, Ahmadinejad, & the 12th Imam," http://www.arewelivinginthelastdays. com/com/iran.html.
19 "Signs of the Reappearance of the Twelfth Imam," Books on Islam and Muslims, Al-Islam.org.

Israel in the Gog/Magog war, then Iran will see this as the best opportunity to engage in a war that will call the 12th Imam out of hiding. If Gog suffers defeat in the Gog/Magog war, then so much the better for Iran, because this will pave the way for the appearance of their hidden Imam. Because of these facts, Iran will join in the Gog/Magog war.

It's not hard to imagine the Islamic nations of Sudan and Libya joining the call by Gog to attack Israel. They are both Sunni Muslim nations and will be eager to follow the directions of the new caliph to demonstrate their loyalty to him. They will amass their forces and prepare to attack.

Gog now sees the ideal conditions to secretly attack Israel. He doesn't want to give the Jewish people any warning because their conventional weapons are still quite formidable. But he is confident in their ability to completely annihilate Israel, because the Jewish state's nuclear weapons have been neutralized by mandates from the UN. Gog has overwhelming numerical superiority over the IDF, and because of the element of surprise, the IDF can't mobilize quickly enough to counter the attack of such a huge army coming against them. Israel is doomed. All things are working in Gog's favor as he prepares to launch his attack. His forces gather, and the seconds tick down to the fateful moment. Everyone is in position, everyone is prepared to strike.

Gog will now demonstrate the power of the caliphate. Abu Bakr al-Baghdadi may have resurrected the beast, but Gog will control it as he unleashes the forces of destruction, and this time nothing that man can do will stop it.

The Heavens Watch

While Gog rages and puts his plan into effect to destroy the Jewish people, the Lord watches from the heavens. Something is happening with His people, something He said would happen long ago. They are turning back to Him and acknowledging their offence against Him. In different areas of the Promised Land prayers are offered up to Jehovah. They are fervent prayers, sincere prayers, and prayers pleading for God's intervention. They are contrite prayers with a common theme; they are prayers of repentance with the following words being said over and over again:

> Blessed is he that cometh in the name of the Lord.
> Blessed is he that cometh in the name of the Lord.
> Lord God Almighty,
> Blessed is he that cometh in the name of the Lord.

The *Transcendent Event* is beginning.

Chapter Twelve

CONDITIONS IN ISRAEL BEFORE THE GOG MAGOG WAR

Just before Gog unleashes his forces in the Gog/Magog war, Israel will be experiencing a unique set of circumstances. It might be helpful to review the new reality in Israel so we can understand the situation the Jewish people are dealing with.

- They will have a country that is substantially larger because of the land gained from the Psalm 83 war.

- Israel's new borders will place new security concerns on the IDF.

- Israel will be condemned by the International community because of their use of Nuclear Weapons to defend themselves.

- The UN will impose sanctions on Israel prohibiting future use of Nuclear Weapons. If the Jewish nation uses Nuclear Weapons again, they

will have Nuclear Weapons launched at them.
Israel's Samson Option will be removed.

- Anti-Semitism will rise to new heights. Many Jews will come home to Israel to escape the persecution and help rebuild the nation.

- A new caliphate will be established in Turkey, replacing the counterfeit caliphate of ISIS through Abu Bakr al-Baghdadi.

- Gog will be the leader of the new Turkish caliphate.

- Turkey will emerge as the new power of Islam in the Middle East.

- Turkey will be the power base of the Gog/Magog coalition.

- Israel will enjoy a period of relative peace because their hostile neighbors have been removed from within their country.

- Israel's peace will be short lived because of the new threats of the caliph against them.

- Israel will begin turning back to the Lord in response to the world's animosity toward them.

- Because of the loss of their nuclear weapons, Israel's might will be reduced to conventional weapons that will not be able to repel any large scale invasion.

- Many in Israel will acknowledge their offense against God and will say what Jesus said they would have to say before He turns His face towards them again, "Blessed is he that cometh in the name of the Lord." (Matthew 23:39)

This is a recap of the situation in Israel just prior to the Gog/Magog war. What we have not yet discussed is the biblical precedent for the Gog/Magog war. Just like the Psalm 83 war had a biblical precedent in ancient times, the Gog/Magog war of Ezekiel 38 and 39 has a precedent in ancient times also. That precedent is centered on the time when Sennacherib moved his massive army against the Jewish people, intent on destroying them in their capitol city of Jerusalem.

Sennacherib's move against Jerusalem was the second war in the ancient wars moving to destroy the Jewish people. As you recall from our summary earlier, Sennacherib's army surrounded Jerusalem intent on destroying the Jews. The Jewish King Hezekiah recognized their peril, repented and prayed to the Lord (2 Kings 19:1, 14-19).

The Lord heard Hezekiah's prayers and sent word to him from Isaiah that the Lord would intervene. "That night the angel of the Lord went out and put to death a hundrend and eighty-five thousand in the Assyrian camp." (2 Kings 19:35 NIV) God used heavenly intervention to accomplish His purposes. It was not by the hand of men that the city of Jerusalem was saved, it was by the hand of the Lord. God intervened, and the Jewish people were saved.

If the Gog/Magog war is to follow the precedent set in ancient times, then Israel will not be saved this time by the hands of the Israeli Defense Force. They will be saved by direct heavenly intervention. The Lord is going to do something by His hand, not by the actions of man, to intervene and destroy the armies of the Gog coalition. When God does this, the entire world is going to tremble. The Lord is going to make a statement by His actions—the statement will be impossible to ignore. All those who try to destroy His people Israel will themselves be destroyed. God is going to be furious with those leading the charge to annihilate the house of Israel.

Leading the charge into the fury of the Lord will be the man, the caliph, Gog.

Chapter Thirteen

THE SECOND WAR IN ISRAEL'S FUTURE, THE GOG AND MAGOG WAR

And so it begins. Gog has amassed his forces and comes against the modern day nation of Israel. This is the coalition described in Ezekiel thirty eight. Israel is not expecting this attack and has recently been living in relative peace, existing safely in their land.

Ezekiel describes Gog rising up to come into the land of Israel. "In the latter years thou shalt come into the land that is brought back from the sword, and is gathered out of many people, against the mountains of Israel, which have been always waste: but it is brought forth out of the nations, and they shall dwell safely all of them." (Ezekiel 38:8)

The fact that Israel is unprepared for this attack is reinforced when Ezekiel points out that the inhabitants of Israel will be "at rest" and "dwelling safely" in their land of "unwalled villages."

"And thou shalt say, I will go up to the land of unwalled villages; I will go to them that are at rest, that dwell safely, all of them dwelling without walls, and having neither bars nor gates." (Ezekiel 38:11)

Gog is going to bring a vast army with him. "Thou shalt ascend and come like a storm, thou shalt be like a cloud to cover the land, thou and all thy bands, and many people with thee." (Ezekiel 38:9)

We need a point of clarification because this is an important issue. The Gog and Magog war is clearly a time when Israel is not expecting an attack. It differs from the end time Battle of Armageddon because during Armageddon, Israel will be battle-hardened and reeling from many years of constant harassment by the world's forces. They will expect to be attacked during the battle of Armageddon. In fact, being attacked constantly will be common place during that precarious time. This fact places the Gog/Magog war at a different time than Armageddon.

What will be Gog's purpose for attacking Israel? The Bible says that Gog will be coming to take plunder (a spoil), to enslave people (prey), to take silver and gold, and to take cattle and goods.

"Art thou come to take a spoil? Hast thou gathered thy company to take a prey? To carry away silver and gold, to take away cattle and goods, to take a great spoil?" (Ezekiel 38:13)

Gog will be treating Israel like it has no right to exist and should be wiped off the face of the earth. This has constantly been the position of Islam ever since the inception of Israel in May of 1948. Gog will reinforce this position to the extreme and will try to get the world to follow him to completely destroy the nation of Israel.

The thing that Gog and his hordes never counted on is the Lord's reaction to their invasion of His land to destroy His people. Gog is going to experience something few people have ever endured in our day and age. The Lord will tolerate many things that people do, but He will not tolerate the total and wanton destruction of His people that have been gathered out of the nations into His land. The Lord is going to be furious with the invading army foolish enough to attack the land of His chosen people. Gog and his army are going to be decimated by the onslaught of the Lord in His anger. The Bible makes this clear in the following verse:

"And it shall come to pass at the same time when Gog shall come against the land of Israel, saith the Lord God, that my fury shall come up in my face." (Ezekiel 38:18)

The Lord is going to act to destroy Gog and his armies—and He is going to do it by supernatural intervention from Heaven. The Bible tells us this and describes exactly how He will accomplish the destruction of Gog and his armies. First the Bible tells us that there is going to be a cataclysmic earthquake—one so gigantic that it will be felt by all people on the face of the earth:

"For in my jealousy and in the fire of my wrath have I spoken, Surely in that day there shall be a great shaking in the land of Israel, So that the fishes of the sea, and the fowls of the heaven, and the beasts of the field, and all creeping things that creep upon the earth, and all the men that are upon the face of the earth, shall shake at my presence, and the mountains shall be thrown down, and the steep places shall fall, and every wall shall fall to the ground." (Ezekiel 38:19-20)

This is not going to be a typical regional earthquake, but will be a worldwide earthquake felt by everyone living on the face of the earth. No one will be safe from this earthquake. It will impact "all men" and every fish, bird and creature on the face of the earth. It's as if our Lord is shaking the world to try to get our attention—to see if we will pay attention to what is going on. He will also be demonstrating to Gog that he will not succeed.

What occurs next will be just as alarming. The Lord will use supernatural intervention to destroy Gog and all but one sixth of his massive army. The Lord is marshalling His weapons of destruction to accomplish His purpose. These weapons will come from the sky and will pummel the earth and mountains where Gog's hordes are massing for their attack. The Bible tells us this in the following verse:

"And I will plead against him with pestilence and with blood; and I will rain upon him, and upon his bands, and upon the many people that are with him, an overflowing rain, and great hailstones, fire, and brimstone." (Ezekiel 38:22)

What are the great hailstones, fire and brimstone that the Lord is talking about in this passage? This Scripture is not talking about the normal rain that we are familiar with. Instead, what is being described is a more appropriate description of meteorites and volatile materials falling from the skies and igniting a conflagration in the fire that ensues. How can something falling from the sky do that?

It's not as difficult as it might seem when we consider the materials existing in space in our solar system or the materials comprising the interstellar medium. This is a rain that is comprised of volatile materials that are routinely found in the interstellar medium or in a comet's debris field. Countless comets have come into our solar system through the ages and leave vast swaths of space littered with their debris. These debris fields are usually no longer visible to the naked eye.

Many astronomers have done extensive analysis of these debris fields and the interstellar medium in space and have found an abundance of complex volatile materials (materials containing carbon).[20] In fact, almost half of the substances found in space are volatile when combined with oxygen in the air. If any of these volatile materials were to come into contact with the atmosphere of the earth, all you would need is some oxygen and a spark and you could ignite an inferno. There would be literal sheets of fire falling from the skies. The atmosphere supplies the oxygen, and the spark could come from meteors as they become red-hot and streak across the sky.

This, or something like it, may be what the Lord meant when he describes the abnormal rain, the fire, hailstones and brimstone that fall from the sky. If that is the case, then we should find some evidence to support this "fire from the sky" conclusion. Again, in Ezekiel 39:6, the Lord repeats, "And I will send a fire on Magog...."

The Lord does not use bombs or modern weapons to accomplish His purposes, but has a far more effective method to carry out His will. He uses materials that are readily available to Him from His creation in the interstellar and solar medium. Vast quantities of complex volatile materials entering our oxygen-rich atmosphere would burst into flame to become the "fire" that will fall on Gog and Magog, slaughtering his armies.

After Gog's armies are destroyed, we are told that Israel will burn the weapons of his armies for seven years, using them as fuel. "Then those who live in the towns of Israel will go out and use the weapons for fuel and burn them up—the small and large shields, the bows and arrows, the war clubs and spears. For seven years they will use them for fuel. They will not need to gather wood from the fields or cut it from the forests, because they will use the weapons for fuel. And they will plunder those who plundered them and loot those who looted them, declares the Sovereign

---

20 Carl Sagan, Ann Druyan, *Comet*, (New York, NY: Pocket Books, 1985), pp.150-151.

Lord." (Ezekiel 39:9-10 NIV) Another reason they won't need any wood to burn the weapons is because all they need for the fire is already there. Not all of the volatile material will burn up while falling to the ground when Gog's armies are destroyed. Vast quantities of the petroleum like substance will still be lying on the ground, ready to fuel the fires that will destroy the remnants of Gog's weapons. No wood will be necessary.

A similar passage from Isaiah also warns of God's supernatural intervention: "The noise of a multitude in the mountains, like as of a great people; a tumultuous noise of the kingdoms of nations gathered together: The Lord of hosts mustereth the host of the battle. They come from a far country, from the end of heaven, even the Lord, and the weapons of his indignation, to destroy the whole land. Howl ye; for the day of the Lord is at hand; it shall come as a destruction from the Almighty." (Isaiah 13:4-6)

There are several observations that we can make from this passage. First, the Lord is using an army gathered from the ends of heaven, something that no man is able to do. The weapons of His indignation come from heaven and will destroy the land, and will come as a destruction from the Almighty. This is not man launching missiles, but the Lord using His heavenly soldiers armed with heavenly weapons. There is also a point made in this Scripture that we might easily overlook if we are not paying attention. It says "the day of the Lord is at hand."

This point is critical when establishing the timing of the event that leads to the destruction of Gog's army. When the Scripture says "the day of the Lord is at hand," it means the day of the Lord is going to begin immediately following the destruction of Gog's army. The "Day of the Lord" is a critical term to understand and accurately pinpoints the exact time we are in on God's timetable.

We will discuss this in depth later but for now let's look at the fate of those forces in the Gog and Magog alliance.

The Fate of Gog and His Alliance

The massive army that Gog has raised and used to attack the nation of Israel will be destroyed. There will only be a sixth part of it left. "And I will turn thee back, and leave but the sixth part of thee." (Ezekiel 39:2)

Gog's fate will be equally devastating. "And I will smite thy bow out of thy left hand, and will cause thine arrows to fall out of thy right hand. Thou shalt fall upon the mountains of Israel, thou, and all thy bands, and the people that is with thee: I will give thee unto the ravenous birds of every sort, and to the beasts of the field to be devoured." (Ezekiel 39:3-4)

Gog will die, along with most of his army; and they shall become a feast for the birds and beasts of the field. There is an interesting phrase used before Gog is killed. It says Gog will have the "bow smitten out of his left hand." An interesting parallel is that the first horseman of the apocalypse, the rider on the white horse, will have a bow in his hand, and he will go forth conquering and to conquer just like Gog. (Revelation 6: 2)

Gog and his multitudes will be buried in Israel in the valley of Hamon-gog. "And it shall come to pass in that day, that I will give unto Gog a place there of graves in Israel, the valley of the passengers on the east of the sea; and it shall stop the noses of the passengers: and there shall they bury Gog and all his multitude: and they shall call it The valley of Hamon-gog." (Ezekiel 39:11)

It will take seven months to bury all those killed in the Gog/Magog coalition. "And seven months shall the house of Israel be burying of them, that they may cleanse the land." (Ezekiel 39: 12)

This is the end of Gog and the coalition of nations that will come against the land of Israel to destroy it. The Lord again uses the Law of Immediate Recompense in dealing with Gog and the multitudes that joined him to destroy Israel. Their intent and purpose was to destroy Israel, and God turns their evil plan back upon their own heads. They are destroyed instead of Israel, and this time God uses his own hand to carry out their destruction.

The Gog and Magog war also fits the biblical pattern set in ancient times. God has directly intervened to save the modern day nation of Israel, just as he intervened to save ancient Israel when they were surrounded by enemies.

Another chapter has ended in the saga for Israel to fulfill its prophetic destiny. The final chapter is beginning, and this time Israel will face an enemy more cunning and diabolical than any they have faced in the past. This is the time of the advent of the Anti-Christ, and he will shake Israel to their very foundation and leave them guessing whether he was the one promised so long ago.

The *Transcendent Event* will be delayed no longer, the *Transcendent Event* has begun.

Chapter Fourteen

THE TRANSCENDENT EVENT

Throughout the pages of this work, I've mentioned the term *Transcendent Event*. It has been looming in the background, but I haven't explained it yet. *The Transcendent Event* is crucial to our understanding of everything that happens from this point on in this story. It will change everything that we know about our world today, and how our world has been functioning. God will bring about this Transcendent Event and will change the way He operates in the world. Our lives will not be the same after it manifests. For those who do not recognize it, or ignore, or disregard it, their lives will spiral downward to a place from which they may not be able to recover. In short, the Transcendent Event is a paradigm shift of immense proportions, and it all begins with the people that God has chosen to call His own.

What is the *Transcendent Event*? It is best described in a place where we would probably never think to look for it. It appears at the end of the Scripture describing the Gog and Magog war. In order that we may be able to understand this concept, we need to review the passages that refer to the *Transcendent Event*. They are found in the Book of Ezekiel, in the thirty-ninth chapter. The following is from the NIV version of the Bible:

"I will display my glory among the nations, and all the nations will see the punishment I inflict and the hand I lay upon them. From that day forward the house of Israel will know that I am the Lord their God. And the nations will know that the people of Israel went into exile for their sin, because they were unfaithful to me. So *I hid my face from them* and handed them over to their enemies, and they all fell by the sword. I dealt with them according to their uncleanness and their offenses, and *I hid my face from them*. Therefore this is what the Sovereign Lord says: I will now bring Jacob back from captivity and will have compassion on all the people of Israel, and I will be zealous for my holy name. They will forget their shame and all the unfaithfulness they showed toward me when they lived in safety in their land with no one to make them afraid. When I have brought them back from the nations and have gathered them from the countries of their enemies, I will show myself holy through them in the sight of many nations. Then they will know that I am the Lord their God, for though I sent them into exile among the nations, I will gather them to their own land, not leaving any behind. I will no longer hide my face from them, for I will pour out my Spirit on the house of Israel, declares the Sovereign Lord." (Ezekiel 39:21-29 NIV)

The *Transcendent Event* is this: God is no longer going to hide His face from the house of Israel because of their transgressions toward Him. The Lord is going to turn His face, His attention and His focus back on the house of Israel. He is going to pour out His Spirit upon them, and they are going to turn away from their misdeeds and unfaithfulness that they have showed toward the Lord. The house of Israel is going to become the people that the Lord envisioned when he set them apart to Himself. The Lord will be their God, and the house of Israel will be His people. This is the event that will transcend everything we know about how the world operates today.

The phrase "I hid my face from them" has major implications. What does this expression mean? The Lord's act of hiding His face is an expression of divine displeasure. In the Psalms when David sinned, he asked, "How long wilt thou forget me, O Lord? Forever? How long wilt thou hide thy face from me?" (Psalms 13:1)

When the Lord hid his face from David, David was distraught and felt abandoned by the Lord. He felt sorrow in his heart and his enemies triumphed over him. When David felt the Lord's face shine upon him, his disposition completely changed as evidenced by the following passage in the Psalms. "There be many that say, who will shew us any good? Lord, lift thou up the light of thy countenance upon us. Thou hast put gladness in my heart, more than in the time that their corn and their wine increased. I will both lay me down in peace, and sleep: for thou, Lord, only makest me dwell in safety." (Psalms 4:6-8)

David was happy and had gladness and peace in his heart when the Lord's countenance shown upon him. When the Lord hides His face, bad things happen to people. When God shines His face toward someone, they are happy and have gladness and peace in their heart. The house of Israel will experience a major transformation when the Lord no longer hides His face from them.

When God hid His face from the house of Israel, they suffered tremendously. They lost their national sovereignty and went into captivity. Following their captivity, they lived as a vassal state to the Romans, subject to Rome while in their own land. A few years after Jesus death, the Romans destroyed Jerusalem and the Jewish people were dispersed throughout the world again. They suffered a tremendous holocaust in the nations where they resided and millions of them lost their lives. They lost their rights as citizens in various nations, had their property and possessions seized, and became a derogatory term in the eyes of many people. The only thing they didn't lose was their ethnic identity.

Now God has gathered them again in their land and has been watching over them since that time. But as of yet, the Lord has not turned His face and focused all of his attention on Israel. At the end of the Gog and Magog war, everything changes just as the Lord said it would. The house of Israel will no longer be handed over to their enemies, and He will pour out His Spirit on the entire house of Israel. They will begin to trust in Him again, and learn to call on the Lord in their times of trouble. They will be blessed of the Lord, just like many of us have been throughout the years. The blessings that have flowed so freely to us will now be focused on the house of Israel as well. They will be the apple of His eye as the church has been for almost two thousand years.

In writing these things, I couldn't help but be resentful that we must share the focus of God's attention. I know I should be happy for the house of Israel, but my human nature was interfering with the joy and happiness that I should feel for them. A certain amount of resentment overtook me as I thought about the real life implications of this. We, the church, and those that love the Lord must share the attention shown primarily to us with the house of Israel, much like an only child when they discover they must share their parents' attention when a new sibling arrives. This almost seemed not fair in my perspective of things. Didn't God realize everything we had done for Him when Israel had ignored Him? Didn't the Lord realize how we had sacrificed and struggled to do the right things, and had many times suffered from doing what He asked of us? How could this be fair that the Lord would show the same care and attention to the house of Israel when we had always been there for Him, even before they began to turn back to Him?

As I pondered these things and felt sorry for myself, I voiced my concerns to God in prayer. It wasn't until I calmed down and was still that I got my answer. It was almost imperceptible at first, but then an overwhelming feeling of peace and calm overcame me as I heard an answer to my prayer. I heard the Spirit speak clearly to me in my mind.

The Lord's Answer to Prayer

"Don't you know that I will always love you? Don't you know that you will always be mine? I was there during the times in your life when you thought you couldn't go on, when you felt that all was lost, and life could never get better again. I was there when you were betrayed, and thrown away by those who you thought loved you. I was there when you suffered from the loss of your loved ones, a loss so terrible it left a void that you felt could never be filled. I was there when you felt no one could love you, and no one could see you for who you are. I was there in the bounds of loneliness, in your time of despair, and I was there in the times of your triumph, and in the times when you felt no one could stop you."

"You are loved more than you could ever know, more than you ever thought possible. You will never be separated from me, and at the proper time I will send my angels and you will be gathered home to me. I have prepared a mansion for you that you will not believe even if I were to describe it to you."

"In the times of your troubles you always turned back to me, and trusted in me even though you did not understand what I was doing. I remember when you were so angry that you would not talk to me, the times when you questioned all that I allowed to happen in your life. Still, you had faith in me, and always returned to the path that I had set you on and asked of you. Your faith increased and you trusted me even in the bad times of the night seasons, when you could not see clearly out of the dark tunnel you were in. Your faith triumphed when all things seemed to conspire against you, and you kept your eye on me and held fast in times of adversity, knowing that somehow I would make all things work together for your good."

"You went out and did the things that I asked of you, even though many times no one saw your efforts for others but me. You were overlooked while the praise went to others, you carried on when no one else would, and you persevered when others stopped trying and gave up. I saw your effort on my behalf and I look forward to the time when I can say to you, 'Well done my good and faithful servant; your reward is waiting for you in heaven'."

"You have accepted the free gift offered to all, the sacrifice of my Son so that He could take on your sins so that you can be with me. You have recognized the only way you can be with me and I will gladly welcome you into my kingdom. Now go and do as I ask of you, and when the time is right, I will bring you home to me; and from that point and evermore you will always be with me. Carry on until I send for you, and be still and know that I am God."

A response like this always puts things in perspective. Those who have accepted Jesus Christ into their lives, acknowledged their sins, and asked for Christ's saving blood to cover their sins are never going to be separated from God. The Lord will bring them home when the time is right. (The Rapture) He will send his angels to get them, and we will be with Him forevermore. Israel will need to be the focus of His attention because they will still be present on the earth when we have been raptured and are with the Lord in Heaven.

Because of this fact, we should be happy. The Lord will need to turn his face toward Israel so they can endure all the things that are going to happen to them. Without God's protection, they would never survive. *The Transcendent Event* will protect them, just as it will protect us. We will be taken home, and the house of Israel will have God's full attention.

They will need it, because waiting in the shadows is the greatest challenge the world will ever know. A man will arise saying that he is god, and that he is the one that protected Israel from complete and total annihilation. He will take credit for what God has done, and he will rise to power promising peace to everyone. He will be the solution to the peace problem in the Middle East, and he will have the perfect plan for implementing that peace. All that Israel will have to do is to trust in him and sign a document promising peace to their war torn nation. Then their problems will be over. This will be the greatest lie ever fabricated in the history of mankind.

This will be the promise of the one that will be known as the antichrist.

Chapter Fifteen

PRELUDE TO THE RISE OF THE ANTICHRIST

How does the antichrist rise to power? How is it possible that the Islamic world suffers two horrendous defeats and yet seemingly out of nowhere a man arises from the ashes of those defeats and ascends to become the leader that many in the world adore? His advent is the most unlikely of scenarios, unless you understand what is going on in the background and why God allows it to happen. In order to understand how the antichrist comes to power, we need to examine the new reality in the world at the conclusion of the conflict where Gog and his forces were defeated. Let's summarize the new condition of the world.

- Israel had defeated ISIS and the counterfeit caliph previously, and with heavenly intervention from the Lord. The armies of the caliph, Gog, that arose from many people has been defeated and lies moldering on the plains of Israel.

- Israel is still alive and well living in the borders of the land that the Lord has granted them, stretching from the Nile River to the River Euphrates.

- Israel has survived two attempts to destroy them. They are saved by the use of nuclear weapons deployed by the IDF in the first attempt. In the second attempt by the armies of Gog and Magog they are saved by God's direct intervention using divine means.

- The nation of Israel is hated by the world because of their use of nuclear weapons in the Psalm 83 war, and because they survived when the armies of the caliph, Gog, were destroyed along with the Magog armies.

- The nation of Turkey has been seriously weakened because of the defeat of the armies that arose from within its borders that followed Gog.

- Turkey, the nation that was home of the legitimate caliph for over 500 years, and the home of the recent caliphate led by Gog, is no longer in control of the office of the caliph because Gog was killed on the plains of Israel.

- A power vacuum has been created by the loss of the legitimate caliphate that was formerly in Turkey.

- The nation of Israel is reeling from the constant state of war, and is willing to recognize almost anyone that can give them the assurance of peace.

- The stage is set for a new leader to come on the scene; a leader that comes to power through promises of peace, instead of the call for war.

- The time is ripe for the advent of the antichrist.

These are the conditions in the Middle East at the conclusion of the second war to fulfil Israel's prophetic destiny. What are the conditions in the rest of the world during this time? Why does the antichrist arise to power so easily and so unopposed while the rest of the world is watching?

The answer to that question can be found when we carefully examine the details of what happens during the Gog/Magog war. This war is not some insignificant little event, or some occurrence that only impacts the area of the Middle East. This war has worldwide consequences, and the nations of the world will be reeling from what happens. What is it about this war that would cause such worldwide disruption?

The answer to that question is an earthquake; an earthquake that is so immense it affects everyone on the face of the earth. This is not a normal earthquake, but an earthquake that shakes all portions of the globe at once. No one is spared from this earthquake, because the Lord is furious with the world for trying to destroy His covenant people. The Lord is going to shake the entire world to try to get our attention, and the description of this earthquake is almost mind boggling. The description of it is found in the thirty eighth chapter of Ezekiel:

"And it shall come to pass at the same time when Gog shall come against the land of Israel, saith the Lord God, that my fury shall come up in my face. For in my jealousy and in the fire of my wrath have I spoken, Surely in that day there shall be a great shaking in the land of Israel; so that the fishes of the sea, and the fowls of the heaven, and the beasts of the field, and all creeping things that creep upon the earth, and all the men that are upon the face of the earth, shall shake at my presence, and the mountains shall be thrown down, and the steep places shall fall, and every wall shall fall to the ground." (Ezekiel 38: 18-20)

Everything will be affected by this worldwide earthquake. The fish of the sea, the birds of the heavens, the beasts of the field, every creeping thing, and "all men that are upon the face of the earth" are going to feel this earthquake. This is an earthquake so large that the Richter scale will have a hard time measuring it. The devastation caused by this earthquake is going to be almost incalculable. Mountains will be thrown down, and walls will fall to the ground.

Let's try to imagine the effect an earthquake of this magnitude will have on the world. First and foremost, cataclysmic Tsunamis will be generated in the oceans around the world. Every costal city on the earth is going to be affected. Huge tsunamis will devastate the shoreline cities as massive walls of water sweep inland destroying everything in their path. All areas on the coastline of the entire world will be affected.

If mountains are going to be thrown down, and walls are going to collapse all over the earth, the effect this earthquake will have on large buildings in cities and other locations will be catastrophic. All but the most earthquake proof buildings are going to be susceptible to collapse. With all of this devastation, the electrical grid will fail, and conditions will become appalling on every continent.

The infrastructure will be severely damaged, and transportation will be compromised and many roads will become impassable. Life will become a hell on earth.

What could possibly cause an earthquake of this size and magnitude? While the text says that it is the Lord shaking the earth, the way the Lord accomplishes this is described in Isaiah. This Scripture even describes the multitudes of a great people in the mountains gathered together, just as Gog will command his forces to be gathered together for an attack on Israel.

"The noise of a multitude in the mountains, like as of a great people; a tumultuous noise of the kingdoms of nations gathered together: the Lord of hosts mustereth the host of the battle." (Isaiah 13:4)

The hosts of Gog are gathered, ready to strike at Israel, and the Lord brings forth His response to this massive army. He has gathered weapons from the end of heaven, and they become the weapons of His indignation.

"They come from a far country, from the end of heaven, even the Lord, and the weapons of his indignation, to destroy the whole land." (Isaiah 13:5)

What is God bringing from the far reaches of space that brings destruction on the world? The Bible does not give us a clear explanation of how the Lord accomplishes this feat but many biblical scholars have put forth some theories on how this might occur. Two of those scholars are Imanuel Velikovsy and Donald Wesley Patten. Velikovsky's book, *Worlds in Collision*, was a ground-breaking work that detailed how many events in the Bible could be attributed to the earth having planetary close encounters with other large bodies in space. Donald Wesley Patten refined some of this work in his book, *Catastrophism And The Old Testament*, and describes the precise orbital dynamics that would produce the effects being described in many Scriptures. While it is true that their work is highly speculative, their conclusions are based on the facts presented in the Bible and may provide the means by which the Lord accomplishes His will.

The scenario that Isaiah presents sounds like a planetary close encounter of some kind, much like Velikovsky and Patten have proposed. There are a huge variety of objects present in space, from sizes ranging from small meteors, to comet-sized bodies, to planet-sized objects all throughout our solar system and beyond. If a large-sized interplanetary body came anywhere near the earth, we would have the exact conditions being described in these Scriptures. The pull of the gravitational field from the other large body in space would cause immense disruption of the crustal plates of the earth, upon which every continent and city lies. This would lead to cataclysmic earthquakes, and if the interplanetary body came close enough to earth, the earthquake caused could be truly immense. This is precisely what we see in the description in Ezekiel. Ezekiel describes an earthquake so large that it impacts the whole world.

What happens next after the description of the earthquake in Ezekiel would tend to support our conclusion and the Lord's description of something brought from the outer reaches of our solar system. As the large interplanetary body passes by the earth, the earth enters into the debris field trailing in the wake of the huge object. All the vast quantities of volatile gases and rocks and meteors are pulled into the earth's atmosphere and begin plunging down on the surface of the world.

If you remember, Gog and his armies are going to be destroyed by huge hail like objects and sheets of fire, an overflowing rain of fire and brimstone falling out of the sky. A close encounter of our planet passing close by a large interplanetary body would produce the exact effect being described by Ezekiel. Gog and his armies are going to be immolated in this encounter, and the rest of the world is going to be devastated by the earthquake.

If the earthquake is large enough, and the gravitational pull of the object passing by the earth is strong enough, it could disrupt the orbit of our planet. In the same chapter in Isaiah where it describes the Lord marshalling the weapons of His indignation, it also describes a disruption in the planetary orbit of earth. "Therefore I will shake the heavens, and the earth shall remove out of her place…" (Isaiah 13:13)

This effect of the earth moving out of its place could shorten the orbit of the earth, and return the earth to an orbit of 360 days a year, which most experts agree was the former orbital duration of the earth based on ancient calendars in the past. The fact that the earth's days are going to be shortened is reinforced in the gospels of Matthew and Mark where both gospels say that "for the elect's sake those days shall be shortened." (Matthew 24:22) (Mark 13:20) No longer will the earth have an orbit around the sun of 365¼ days, but it will be 360 days a year, as it was in ancient times.[21]

A Brief Review

Let's take a few moments and review what we have discussed so far. A great earthquake is going to strike the earth sometime in the near future. It will occur when the caliphate under the leadership of Gog from Turkey is amassing a huge army to attack Israel. The effects of this earthquake will be felt by everyone on the face of the earth. Mass destruction and devastation will come as a result of this global earthquake. Tsunamis will inundate the coastline cities and walls and buildings will collapse all over the world. The electrical grid will be severely disrupted from the destruction

21 Donald Wesley Patten, *Catastrophism and the Old Testament* (Seattle, WA: Pacific Meridian Publishing Company, 1988), pp. 221-222.

caused by the earthquake, and there will be failures in the infrastructure as bridges collapse and roads become impassable from the debris littering them. This will be a horrible time to endure.

Gog and his armies will be destroyed from sheets of fire and hail like stones falling out of the sky, the aftereffect of something being brought from the far reaches of our solar system and interacting with the earth. The earth will reel from the encounter with the celestial body passing near it, and the orbit of the earth will be disrupted, causing the earth to settle into a slightly shorter orbit of 360 days a year. The world will be in total chaos from the aftereffect of the global earthquake. Darkness will settle over the land as debris from the destruction begins to blacken the light of the sun, and the debris in the air will cause the moon to turn into a blood-like color.

A Question to Ponder

I have to ask a question of all those who are reading this. Does this sound like a time you want to be involved in? Is there anything even remotely appealing about what has been described above? To any rational person, this is a time to be avoided at all costs. Death and destruction will become commonplace during this event; the world as we knew it will cease to be. Everything is going to change from this point in time. Nothing will be the same again.

The logical question then becomes: What will happen to us? What will happen to those of us who have accepted Jesus Christ as our Savior? What time is this in the great scheme of things?

The answers to these questions may surprise you. The answers to these questions are found in the last book of the Bible. The Book of Revelation holds the key for finding out exactly where we are when these events occur.

It's time to take a look at that now.

Chapter Sixteen

THE TIMING OF THE GREAT EARTHQUAKE

We have just discussed a great earthquake that is going to shake the entire world. This earthquake is so large and so spectacular that it simply has to be mentioned in the Book of Revelation which summarizes end time events. If we can find where this earthquake is mentioned, then this will give us important clues where we are in relation to God's time clock and all the things described in Revelation. Then maybe we can get some idea what is happening at the time of the great earthquake. This will help us focus in on what to expect when the sign of this great earthquake happens.

The Great Earthquake in Revelation

The first time we find a description of a great earthquake in Revelation is in the sixth chapter. The earthquake is described like this:

"And I beheld when he had opened the sixth seal, and lo, there was a *great earthquake*; and the sun became black as sackcloth of hair, and the moon became as blood." (Revelation 6:-12)

This is enlightening because when we see the description of the great earthquake in Revelation, we are already at the point of the sixth seal. Why is this earthquake the same earthquake we see described in Ezekiel? It's because we see that this earthquake initiates the Day of the Lord judgments exactly in the same manner that the earthquake in Ezekiel begins the destructive events. We see the kings of the earth making this point when they say, "For the great day of his wrath is come; and who shall be able to stand?" (Revelation 6:17) The Day of the Lord begins with the destructive events described in the "great earthquake" of Revelation 6:12. Further evidence of this can be seen when the destructive events cause the sun to become black and the moon to turn as blood. All other earthquakes described in Revelation come after the Day of the Lord has begun.

Sometime after the opening of the sixth seal, the sign of a "great earthquake" is given. That gives us an idea of where we are on God's time clock, but what exactly has happened before the sign of the great earthquake was given?

If you go to the beginning of the sixth chapter, you see that the Four Horsemen of the Apocalypse have been released on the earth. Who are the four horsemen of the apocalypse and what do they represent?

The four horsemen are riders that each issue in a specific ordeal that the world will have to endure. Let's take a look at the description of the first horseman. "And I saw, and behold a white horse: and he that sat on him had a bow; and a crown was given unto him: and he went forth conquering, and to conquer." (Revelation 6:2)

What insight can we garner from this passage? The rider on the white horse has a bow, a weapon of war in his hand so he must be involved in wars. He has a crown on his head so he must be someone in authority and a leader of an empire. It also says that he went forth conquering—so that means he is involved in wars where he has defeated some groups of people and has subjugated them. It also says that he is going forth to conquer—so that must mean that there is a group of people that he wants to defeat in battle, but it has not yet happened.

Next we read about the red horse. "And there went out another horse that was red: and power was given to him that sat thereon to take peace from the earth, and that they should kill one another: and there was given unto him a great sword." (Revelation 6:4)

This verse is self-explanatory. The red horse represents war, because peace will be taken from the earth, and everyone will begin to kill each other. This language speaks of another world war that is going to start. The rider on the red horse is an empire that is going to have a great sword in their hand which means they will have the capability to wage war and be successful in this war across the globe.

There is going to be famine throughout the world because of the actions of this empire. It is going to take an entire day's wages just to buy a handful of wheat or barley. Famine will be rampant throughout the world and there will not be enough food being produced to feed everyone. This is a natural result of a war raging where farmers will not be able to till their lands. This is what is being described by the third horseman of the apocalypse. "And when he had opened the third seal, I heard the third beast say, Come and see. And I beheld, and lo a black horse; and he that say on him had a pair of balances in his hand. And I heard a voice in the midst of the four beasts say, A measure of wheat for a penny, and three measures of barley for a penny; and see thou hurt not the oil and the wine." (Revelation 6:5, 6)

The fourth and final horseman is more mysterious. The description given in Revelation is absolutely chilling. "And I looked, and behold a pale horse: and his name that sat on him was Death, and Hell followed with him. And power was given unto them over the fourth part of the earth, to kill with sword, and with hunger, and with death, and with the beasts of the earth." (Revelation 6:8)

As a result of this horseman, over a billion people are going to lose their lives. They are going to be killed during wars, they are going to be captured and starved to death, they are going to be slaughtered by Death and Hell, and they are going to be butchered by the beasts of the earth. The beasts of the earth can include the animals we are familiar with, and probably includes beasts on a microbial scale. Infectious disease pathogens can also be described as beasts when considering all the damage they can do. Diseases such as Ebola, Small Pox, Anthrax and hemorrhagic fevers are probably included in this category also.

Regardless of the means used to carry out their plans, death is going to come to the earth on a scale that has never been seen before.

What insights can we learn from reviewing the four horsemen of the apocalypse? Does what we see here apply to anything else we have reviewed so far? Let's summarize what we have discovered in this review.

- A great earthquake is described in the Book of Revelation and is said to occur during what is described as the sixth seal.

- During the great earthquake, the sun becomes black as sackcloth, and moon becomes as blood.

- Prior to the great earthquake, the four horsemen of the apocalypse are described.

- The four horsemen are described as riders unleashing a series of events in the world.

- The leader (crown) of the empire is a rider on a white horse who has a bow in his hand.

- The leader of the empire has been involved in wars and has conquered many people.

- The leader of the empire has another group that he wants to conquer, but it has not happened yet.

- War is unleashed on the world, war of a global scale by the leader of the empire.

- Famine strikes the world, and people will have to spend a day's wages just to be able to get a handful of food.

The empire is going to employ all means available to it to destroy people. This includes wars, starvation of people, being destroyed by death and hell, and being killed by the beasts of the earth which can also include microbial agents.

This list is appalling and troublesome, but it has not been reproduced in order to disturb you. It has been given so that we can recognize any similarities to someone that we have been discussing. Are there any clues given here to help us identify a leader who will arise; a leader who will control an empire, a leader with a bow in his hand, a leader who will lead his forces in war, forces that are large enough to wage war across the entire world, a leader who will try to conquer the house of Israel and will fail, and a leader who will worship death and hell so much that he loves to see people killed, starved and destroyed?

The person that has the attributes and characteristics of all of these things is the man who will be Gog. Gog is the leader that fits this description to a tee. Gog will be the leader of an empire that can best be described as a "beast." What is a "beast" as described by the Bible? A beast is a group of people or an empire that follows a false religion and is intent on harming other people. The precedent for this is found in Daniel where every mention of the word "beast" refers to an empire or group of people following a false religion that consistently harms other people. (See Daniel 7:5-7)

Why does the description of a rider on a white horse fit Gog? Let's consider the following:

- Gog is the leader (caliph) of a beast empire that will arise in Turkey.

- He replaces a caliphate (Abu Bakr al-Baghdadi, ISIS) who is demonstrating new ways to show man's inhumanity to man.

- Gog will raise these atrocities to new heights in pursuit of his Islamic empire that he wants to rule the world.

- Anyone that will not convert or espouse a belief in Islamic teachings will be killed in the most horrible of ways.

- Gog will wage war by his followers across the world.

- Gog will employ all means possible to carry out destruction across the world, and will manage to kill one fourth of the entire world's population.

Gog fits all of the characteristics of the rider on the white horse that we see when the first seal in the Book of Revelation is opened. He leads a beast empire and is the leader of the caliphate at that time. He unleashes his forces to cause war, famine and death on an unprecedented scale throughout the world. He will be especially brutal to Christians, because they will not submit to him or worship anyone other than Jesus Christ. If you have a testimony of Jesus Christ, then you will become the enemy to Gog and his minions.

Many Christians will be killed during his rampage, and this fact is documented in the passages just before the great earthquake. "And when he had opened the fifth seal, I saw under the altar the souls of them that were slain for the word of God, and for the testimony which they held." (Revelation 6:9)

Our Lord is going to be furious with the treatment and death of Christians. Gog will not be allowed to continue. Gog will have the bow slapped out of his hand. (Ezekiel 39:3) Gog will not be permitted to go forth to conquer Israel. (Ezekiel 39:4)

The Lord is going to personally intervene to destroy Gog. He is going to marshal the weapons of his indignation from the ends of heaven, (Isaiah 13:5) and cause them to fall on Gog. (Ezekiel 39:4) Gog is going to be destroyed by rock like hail and sheets of fire from heaven. (Ezekiel 38:22)

The earth is going to be shaken by a great earthquake because of the death of the martyrs and those who refused to deny their testimony of Jesus Christ. (Revelation 6:9) God's fury is going to be displayed because of the Christians who have been killed, and because of the temerity of those who think that they can destroy the house of Israel. The great earthquake occurs after many

Christians have been killed, and during the time when Gog is moving his forces to destroy Israel.

The Lord loves all of His people, the Christians as well as the house of Israel. The Lord's anger is going to rise up, and He is going to be furious because many Christians have been killed and now His covenant people are threatened. Our God is not going to tolerate this situation any longer. Justice will be tempered by mercy no longer.

Two things are going to happen before the destruction of great earthquake. The first thing is that the house of Israel is going to have 144,000 people, 12,000 from each tribe, sealed for the purpose of serving God. They are going to be set apart and consecrated for service to the Lord.

The second thing that happens will affect everyone who loves the Lord, and does as He asks, and trusts in Jesus Christ as their Savior. The Lord will be bringing us home to Him where we can be protected. He will send His angels to gather us up from all over the face of the earth. We will be caught up to meet the Lord in the Heavens, and we will always be with Him from this point forward.

How is it possible that anyone can know this? Are these conclusions based on wild speculations, or is there someplace in God's Word where we are told these things?

That's the subject of the next chapter.

Chapter Seventeen

THE RAPTURE OF THE CHURCH

How is it possible to know the timeframe on God's clock when the rapture of the church occurs? Is it possible to know something like this? I want everyone to be perfectly clear on the following point. I'm not saying that I know the time or the hour of this event, for nobody can know those things. I am not date setting or even proposing a time. What I am saying is that you can know the conditions that will be prevalent in the world when this event occurs. We can look at certain events as time markers on God's clock. One of the events that will stand out for all to notice is the great earthquake that will strike our world. It is a seminal event, something that delineates a clear change in how things are going to happen on earth.

When the great earthquake strikes, it will herald the start of a time when great destruction will ravage the earth. What may be surprising to many is the fact that the destruction will be orchestrated by the Lord. This is a time period that is going to be known as the Day of the Lord. The great earthquake initiates the time of great destruction (The Day of the Lord) that will begin the time of the end. What happens before the Day of the Lord begins?

If we examine the Scriptures carefully, in the seventh chapter of Revelation, two things are going to happen before destruction is allowed to come upon the earth. First, many people in the house of Israel (144,000) are going to be sealed in their foreheads. And secondly, immediately after that sealing, a great multitude of ethnically diverse people, from every nation, all speaking a variety of different languages; are going to appear in heaven before the throne of Jesus.

Who are these people? Let's take a look at what the Scripture says so we can get clues that will help us identify them.

"After this I beheld, and, lo. A great multitude, which no man could number, of all nations, and kindreds, and people, and tongues, stood before the throne, and before the Lamb, clothed with white robes, and palms in their hands." (Revelation 7:9)

This is a vast amount of people that suddenly appears in heaven, which no man could number. They are from every nation on the earth, from every people, and they speak a variety of different languages. The apostle John seems shocked by their appearance in heaven since they seemed to come out of nowhere. He wonders who these people are and where they came from? He is told the following in response to this question.

"These are they which came out of great tribulation, and have washed their robes, and made them white in the blood of the Lamb." (Revelation 7:14)

The term, "came out of great tribulation," indicates a time when the tribulation the church has normally endured is greatly intensified, and that their sudden appearance represents an escape for this group of people. This would indicate that these people are escaping a time of great destruction, and are being protected and brought home. They are being protected by the Lord from a time when devastation and great tribulation is unleashed on the earth. This is what was promised the church by the rapture. This is the Lord's love and protection manifesting for those who do what God asks of them (are wise) and trust in the Lord.

This group standing before the throne of Jesus Christ is the raptured church. The Lord takes care of them from this point onward. They are not going to be hungry or thirsty any more, and the Lord is going to wipe all their tears from their eyes. No longer is this group going to be persecuted by the world, or suffer at the hands of those that hate the Lord. They are going to be with the Lord from this point forever more.

Many have said that this group represents the martyred saints that were described in the fifth seal; that gave up their lives for their testimony of Jesus Christ, and would not deny Jesus. There is a very important reason that this group cannot be the saints that have been killed for their testimony of Jesus. The people in the group that appears suddenly in Heaven are given palm branches to hold in their hands. That means they are not spirits, but they have actual bodies with hands with which they can hold the palm branches. The saints that have been killed have spiritual bodies, and cannot hold palm branches in their hands because they have not been resurrected yet. Only after they are resurrected will they have actual physical hands with which they can hold things. Therefore, the group that appears suddenly in Heaven has to be **the Raptured Church of Jesus Christ.**

The **Raptured Church of Jesus Christ** appears in Heaven, and the seventh chapter of Revelation says that this happens before the devastation of the great earthquake. "Hurt not the earth, neither the sea, nor the trees, till we have sealed the servants of our God in their foreheads." (Revelation 7:3)

The great earthquake represents the beginning of the Day of the Lord judgments against the earth, and many (the wise in the church doing the will of God and doing what the Lord has asked of them) are going to escape the wrath of God displayed in the Day of the Lord judgments. After we are taken home to be with Jesus, the Day of the Lord begins.

Perhaps it would be helpful to summarize what we have learned so far.

When Gog prepares his massive army to destroy the house of Israel, a global earthquake occurs which is so large that it shakes the entire world.

- The global earthquake during Gog's attack is the same great earthquake described as the sixth seal in the Book of Revelation.

- The Lord is the one causing the great earthquake and He does it by using weapons of His indignation found in the heavens.

- Before the great earthquake is allowed to hurt the earth, the sea and the trees, 144,000 of the house of Israel are sealed and set apart to serve the Lord.

- Before the great earthquake is allowed to take place, the church is raptured and appears in Heaven, to escape persecution and death and to be protected from the destruction and devastation when the wrath of God is unleashed during the Day of the Lord.

- The church age comes to an end because the church has been raptured. (Age of Grace)

- The world will enter a time of judgment, not grace.

- The time of the end of the world begins with the Day of the Lord.

The timing we have just discussed places the rapture of the church before the appearance of the antichrist. There are many that say the rapture of the church does not occur until after the antichrist has appeared on the world scene. They base this assumption on a Scripture found in Second Thessalonians. Let's examine this Scripture and see what the real meaning behind it is and see if we can dispel the confusion. Here is the Scripture:

"Now we beseech you, brethren, by the coming of our Lord Jesus Christ, and by our gathering together unto him." (2 Thessalonians 2:1) Let's stop right here for a moment and examine what has been said. The term, the "coming of our Lord Jesus Christ" refers to the Second Coming of Jesus when he comes to the earth for the second time. This event is depicted in the Scriptures in the nineteen chapter of Revelation. The other term in this verse, "our gathering together unto him" refers to the rapture of the church which takes place at the sixth seal of Revelation, chapter six. Paul is telling us in this verse not to confuse the second coming of Jesus Christ with the rapture of the church—they are two separate and very distinct events.

Let's continue to analyze what has been said. "That ye be not soon shaken in mind, or be troubled, neither by spirit, nor by word, nor by letter as from us, as that the day of Christ is at hand." It's important to note what has just been said here. The term, "the day of Christ" is a reference to the second coming of Jesus Christ. This point is made in the first chapter of Second Thessalonians.

"And to you who are troubled rest with us, when the Lord Jesus shall be revealed from heaven with his mighty angels." (2 Thessalonians 1:7) This is clearly talking about the Second Coming of Jesus Christ when He will be revealed from heaven. The term "in that day" is used later on in this verse in reference to the Second Coming of Jesus. "When he shall come to be glorified in his saints, and to be admired in all them that believe (because our testimony among you was believed) in that day." (2 Thessalonians 1:10) "In that day" is a clear reference to the Second Coming of Christ. It might seem that this point is being over-emphasized, but it is critical to understand what the Scripture is actually saying. The term "in that day" is a clear reference to the Second Coming of Jesus, it doesn't refer to the day of the Lord or any other day.

The reason this is important is because of what the rest of the Scripture says. "Let no man deceive you by any means: for that day [the Second Coming of Jesus Christ] shall not come except there come a falling away first, and that man of sin be revealed [the antichrist], the son of perdition; who opposeth and exalteth himself above all that is called God, or that is worshipped; so that he as God sitteth in the temple of God shewing himself that he is God." (2 Thessalonians 2:3-4)

What this Scripture is saying is that Jesus Christ will not come again the second time (Revelation 19) until the antichrist is revealed and there is a falling away in the church. Many have confused the term "in that day" with the Day of the Lord, and insist that the antichrist has to revealed before the Day of the Lord comes. This is clearly not what the text in Thessalonians says. It is saying that the antichrist must be revealed before the Second Coming, and should not be confused with thinking that the antichrist is going to be revealed before the destruction associated with the Day of the Lord. The Day of the Lord begins with the sixth seal great earthquake, and up until this point in time, the antichrist has not yet made his appearance on the world stage.

This places the rapture of the church before the advent of the antichrist, and before tremendous destruction ravages the face of the earth.

Everything changes when the Lord raptures the church. The end of the world as we know it is beginning. Jesus will be removing His followers to be with Him, and because they have been removed from the earth, the protection bestowed upon the nations will be taken away. The nations will be vulnerable unlike anytime they have ever experienced. The Lord will turn His attention (The Transcendent Event) to the house of Israel. The nations of the world will be left to their own devices for protecting themselves. The protection afforded the nations because of the ones living in them will vanish along with those that are taken into Heaven. It will truly be a time for hell to reign on earth.

And it all starts when the Day of the Lord begins.

Chapter Eighteen

THE DAY OF THE LORD

What exactly is the Day of the Lord? Why is it a time to be avoided? This is something we need to remember: *the Day of the Lord is a time of great destruction upon the earth*. It is a time when the wrath of God is poured out upon the world because of the horrendous treatment of those that bear the name of Christ (Christians) and those trying to destroy the people of God's promise (the house of Israel). It is a time when justice will no longer be tempered with mercy. The age of grace ended when the wise in the church were raptured into Heaven. It is time for judgment. It is a time signaling the end of the world and it all begins with destruction from a great earthquake.

The prophet Joel describes the Day of the Lord in the following way:

"Blow ye the trumpet in Zion, and sound an alarm in my holy mountain: let all the inhabitants of the land tremble: for the day of the Lord cometh, for it is nigh at hand." (Joel 2:1) Notice how the inhabitants of the land tremble—signifying a great earthquake;

and when this sign is given, the Day of the Lord is ready to start. The sign of an earthquake is reinforced later on in this same chapter when it says: "The earth shall quake before them: the heavens shall tremble: the sun and the moon shall be dark and the stars shall withdraw their shining." (Joel 2:10) Notice how similar this language is to the language used to describe the sixth seal where the great earthquake occurs in Revelation. (Revelation 6:12)

Joel is describing the agents (things naturally present in the heavens) the Lord will be using to carry out the destruction, and the agents being used will come as a destruction from the Almighty. "Alas for the day! For the day of the Lord is at hand, and as a destruction from the Almighty shall it come." (Joel 1:15)

Joel describes the Day of the Lord as a day of darkness, gloominess, thick clouds, and a day when tremendous destruction is taking place.

"A day of darkness, and of gloominess, a day of clouds and of thick darkness, as the morning spread upon the mountains: a great people and a strong, there hath not been ever the like, neither shall be any more after it, even to the years of many generations. A fire devoureth before them; and behind them a flame burneth: the land is as the garden of Eden before them, and behind them a desolate wilderness; yea, and nothing shall escape them." (Joel 2:2-3)

The prophet Isaiah paints a very vivid picture of what the Day of the Lord is like. He describes the Day of the Lord and points out that it is caused by the weapons He has gathered from the end of heaven. These are the weapons used to cause the destruction wreaking havoc in the Day of the Lord.

"They come from a far country, from the end of heaven, even the Lord, and the weapons of his indignation, to destroy the whole land. Howl ye; for the day of the Lord is at hand; it shall come as a destruction from the Almighty. Therefore shall all hands be faint, and every man's heart shall melt: And they shall be afraid: pangs and sorrows shall take hold of them; they shall be in pain as a woman that travaileth: they shall be amazed one at another; their faces shall be as flames. Behold the day of the Lord cometh, cruel both with wrath and fierce anger, to lay the land desolate: and he shall destroy the sinners thereof out of it. For the stars of heaven and the constellations thereof shall not give their light: the sun shall be darkened in his going forth, and the moon shall not cause her light to shine. And I will punish the world for their evil, and the wicked for their iniquity; and I will cause the arrogancy of the proud to cease, and will lay low the haughtiness of the terrible." (Isaiah 13:5-11)

Again we see the imagery of darkness and destruction, so much so that the sun and moon will be darkened and cannot be seen. People won't be able to see the stars either. This will most likely be from the clouds and smoke from the destruction taking place on the earth.

God's Word is filled with descriptions of the Day of the Lord, but let's look at another place where it is described in detail. This description is found in Zephaniah, and again a time of destruction and desolation is pointed out.

"The great day of the Lord is near, it is near, and hasteth greatly, even the voice of the day of the Lord: the mighty man shall cry there bitterly. That day is a day of wrath, a day of trouble and distress, a day of wasteness and desolation, a day of darkness and gloominess, a day of clouds and thick darkness." (Zephaniah 1: 14, 15)

I think it is very apparent that the Day of the Lord is a day of destruction, thick clouds, darkness, and gloominess. It is a day that comes as destruction from God, and starts with a great earthquake as we saw in Joel.

Why have we spent so much time on the Day of the Lord? The Day of the Lord represents a radical change in the way God deals with mankind. We are so accustomed to a kind and loving God that we sometimes forget that the Lord will not let sin and wickedness continue on forever. He will deal with them. We also forget that Jesus Christ will be the conquering King when He returns to earth and will be known as the Lion of the tribe of Judah. The Lord is going to be furious with the way both groups of His people have been treated, the Christians and the house of Israel. He has heard the voices of those that have killed asking, "How long, O Lord, holy and true, dost thou not judge and avenge our blood on them that dwell on the earth?" (Revelation 6:10) Jesus Christ is going to wait no longer. He is going to unleash His judgment and the world will tremble when He does. The Lamb has become the Lion of the tribe of Judah.

The Lord has a purpose for unleashing His wrath and judgment upon the world. The primary reason is to protect the house of Israel from complete and total annihilation. This will be the focus of His attention since the wise in the church will have been raptured at this point in time and will be hid away by God until the time of His return. They will be protected securely in heaven while the Lord deals with those that want to destroy His covenant people.

The Lord will protect the house of Israel by destroying Gog and his hordes that are attacking His covenant people. The Magog coalition will fall on the mountains of Israel, hewn down by the Lion of the tribe of Judah. Their surprise attack will not be allowed to succeed, and they will be stopped in their tracks by the Lord. Fire will rain down from heaven upon their heads, and only one sixth of them will survive the Lord's response to their attack.

The world will face a new reality after the destruction of Gog and the start of the Day of the Lord. Here are some of the important points:

- The church will be gone (raptured) from the face of the earth. Only those churches that were not diligent and were not wise in the eyes of the Lord will be left on the earth. The churches left on the earth had a failing evaluation by Jesus because they did not love Christ more than the world, and did not trust in Him enough to do as he asked of them. They have no relationship with Jesus and their faith was insufficient to save them because of their compromise with the world. They are "churches" in name only.

- A global earthquake will shake the world. It will be the largest earthquake ever recorded in the history of mankind. The devastation caused by tsunamis, building collapse, a failing infrastructure and the failure of the electrical grid will be almost incalculable. Untold millions will die.

- There will be so much devastation on the earth that the sun will be obscured to the point that it appears black. The moon will turn to the color of blood before it is totally obscured and people will not be able to see the stars or constellations because of the pollution from the destruction in the air.

- The Lord personally intervened to destroy Gog and his armies. They are lying unburied upon the land of Israel.

- The nation of Israel emerges unscathed from the onslaught. They are protected by the Lord.

- The caliph, Gog, was destroyed. The office of the caliphate has suffered a head wound (the leader) so severe that it is near the point of death. Many in the Islamic religion wonder if the caliphate can ever recover again.

- The religion of Islam has suffered two major defeats with the death of the counterfeit caliph (ISIS, Abu Bakr al-Baghdadi) and the legitimate caliph from Turkey (Gog). The opportunity to hear the Word of God in Muslim countries by those set apart in Israel is opened for millions in the Islamic nations.

- Those in the world surviving the global earthquake and the devastation caused by it are weary of war and the deprivations they have suffered.

- The defeat suffered by Gog and his armies is looked upon by the world as a fulfillment of the Battle of Armageddon. They believe the defeat of Gog was the Battle of Armageddon.

- The world is practically begging for anyone to step up and offer them peace. Anyone promising peace and implementing a way to achieve that peace will be received by the entire world and worshipped as a god, especially now since they think the Battle of Armageddon is over.

- Into the power vacuum and the limelight steps the one that will be revered as a god, the man that will be portrayed as the great peacemaker, the man who is the solution for the world's problems, the man who so many religions are looking forward to with great expectations. The antichrist arises from obscurity.

- The stage is set, and the time is right for the advent of the antichrist. The world thinks the bad times are over. They will soon discover just how wrong they are when this man moves to take over the world, and sets himself up to be the leader of every nation on the planet.

- The time for the antichrist has begun.

Chapter Nineteen

THE BACKGROUND OF THE ANTICHRIST

Who is the antichrist and where does he come from? How does he rise from anonymity to the most prominent position in the world? To find the answers to these questions we need to search the Bible carefully and see what God's Word has to say.

One of the most informative places we can learn about the antichrist is in the Book of Daniel. In the ninth chapter, the antichrist is described as a prince who shall come and establish a peace treaty with the house of Israel for a week of years (seven years). There is a final seven year period of time when Israel will fulfill their prophetic destiny. It is characterized by a peace treaty that the nation of Israel will sign with the antichrist. "And he shall confirm the covenant with many for one week." (Daniel 9:27)

Where does this "prince" promising peace come from? We get our first clue when examining the text in Daniel. "And the people of the prince that shall come shall destroy the city and the sanctuary." (Daniel 9:26)

The "people" of the "prince that shall come" have destroyed the "city" and the "sanctuary." What does this mean? Who are the "people" referenced in this passage, and what city did they destroy, and what is meant by the sanctuary?

In order to uncover the meaning behind this Scripture, we need to review a little history. We need to go to Israel after the time of Jesus's death on the cross. In the year 70 AD, the Roman General Titus led four legions of the Roman army and surrounded the city of Jerusalem. The Jewish people were in rebellion against Roman Rule, and Titus was sent to quell the rebellion. He had his troops surround and lay siege to Jerusalem, and then waited until the Jewish people inside the city were weakened by starvation and deprivation enough that they could be easily conquered.

After waiting until the people of Jerusalem were weakened sufficiently, Titus had the four Roman legions attack. The defenders of Jerusalem were overwhelmed and the city was destroyed so completely that it was merely a shadow of the city it had once been. The temple of the Jewish people, their sanctuary, was burned to the ground and the rock walls that had once been a part of the temple were thrown down, in order to recover the melted gold that was in the crevices. The city of Jerusalem and the temple that had been the heart of the Jewish religion were both destroyed in this attack.

Now we can interpret what the passage in the ninth chapter of Daniel is talking about. The "prince," as we have already discussed, is the antichrist who is going to enforce a peace treaty with the nation of Israel in the last days. The "people" who destroyed Jerusalem and the temple were the people that comprised the four Roman legions. This is an important point because God wants us to recognize who these people are because they are the people of the future antichrist. They are the "people of the prince that shall come." Who were the people that comprised the four Roman legions that destroyed Jerusalem and the temple?

Most people have concluded that because they were Roman legions, the people that destroyed the temple were Europeans. Rome was based in Italy so the logical conclusion is that people of European descent destroyed the city and the sanctuary (temple). While that seems to make perfect sense, is it the correct conclusion to draw from what the Scripture says?

In order to answer that question, we need to examine the ethnic background of the people that comprised the four Roman legions. We also need to remember the following important point— there was an Eastern portion of the Roman Empire that we often overlook. The Eastern portion of the Roman Empire had legions that were comprised of people from the Middle East.

Let's examine the four Roman Legions comprising the army that attacked Jerusalem. Each legion was associated with a number and a name. The tenth (X) legion was called **Fretensis**, and was composed of people from the countries that we now call Turkey and Syria, and also had Nabatean Arabs from West Jordan. This legion was a mixture of Turks, Syrians and Arabs that were Romans, but from the eastern portion of the empire. This was the legion that breached the walls and set fire to the temple.[22]

The next legion was the fifteenth (XV) legion called **Apollinaris**, and was one of the preeminent legions of its day. Josephus, the ancient historian, records that this legion was gathered from cohorts that resided in Syria.

22 Walid Shoebat, Joel Richardson, *God's War on Terror* (New York, NY: Top Executive Media, 2008), p. 352.

History records that the next legion was the twelfth (XII) legion and was called **Fulminata.** Its cohorts were comprised of people from the Melitene region of Eastern Turkey, Syria.

Lastly we have the fifth (V) legion called **Macedonia.** This legion was from the Moesia region in the Balkans south of the Danube River, and was comprised of people from Serbia and Bulgaria.

Altogether, these were the people that made up the Roman legions that destroyed Jerusalem and the temple. They were from the Eastern portion of the Roman Empire and were primarily from the Middle East—Syrians, Turks and Arabs.

Are there any conclusions we can make about these people after we have analyzed where they are from? One thing should be painfully obvious to us all. The countries where these people reside in our day and age are all Islamic countries. They are Muslims and espouse different views of Islam, some Shia and some Sunni, but they are primarily Islamic countries.

With these new facts in mind, we can form some new conclusions based on the analysis we have done. The antichrist (prince) is not of European descent, but comes from the Eastern portion of the Roman Empire, and his people (the people of the prince that shall come) are Islamic and come from Islamic countries.

This is a major paradigm shift for most people watching for the advent of the antichrist. They have been conditioned to believe from popular books and everything that they have seen in the media that the antichrist is going to be a European. Nothing could be further from the truth since an in depth analysis shows that he is going to be a leader of Islamic people, and will get his power base from Muslim nations.

How is it possible that the antichrist arises to power when the office of the caliphate that controls all of Islam, has received a head wound, (the caliphate leader Gog has been recently killed) and teeters on the brink of irrelevance? How does the antichrist resurrect the office of the caliphate, and once again control the beast empire?

The antichrist is going to be the fulfillment of many prophecies and expectations in the Islamic religion. He will be the one that many in the Muslim world are looking for in the end times. He will be the Mahdi that was promised so long ago, the one that Iranian leaders have been trying to force out of hiding.

When he appears, the antichrist will be successful by not making the same mistakes that his predecessors have made. He promises peace where the other caliphs unleashed the dogs of war on the people of the world. What brute force has failed to accomplish, flattery and telling people what they want to hear is going to be successful. The antichrist is going to be charming and will be portrayed as the wisest man the world has ever known. Most likely he will be physically attractive, so much so that most people will believe him to be incapable of tremendous evil. Evil has never been associated with one who is so physically compelling, and the power of his words will mesmerize crowds.

The antichrist will rise to the pinnacle of power, and he does this from a rather inauspicious beginning. The people in the Islamic religion are well acquainted with how he rises to power, but to most of us in the other parts of the world he remains a mystery. It's time to unravel the puzzle that leads to his appearance on the world stage, and learn all we can about the man that comes in like a lamb, but ultimately reveals his true colors as a dragon bent on the subjugation of the entire world.

Chapter Twenty

THE EMERGENCE OF THE TWELFTH IMAM

To understand where the antichrist comes from, we need to know what we don't know about the Islamic religion. In order to do that, we must understand the division of the two main branches of Islam—the Sunni and the Shia. We also need to understand the war that has been going on between these two branches of Islam since the time of Muhammad's death.

Muhammad died in 632 AD and after he died a strong leader rose to take control of the Muslim World. His name was Abu Bakr and he assumed the role of the first caliph. He ruled until 661 AD and after his death a civil war broke out between the Shia and Sunni branches of Islam. There were two different philosophies on the proper governance of all of Islam. The Sunnis felt that the strongest leader should prevail and would be caliph, and the Shias believed that only a direct descendent of Muhammad should be the leader. They called their leader the Imam (one who walks in front).

The Sunni branch of Islam emerged as the stronger of these two branches of Islam, and the caliphs soon began to dominate the control of the Muslim world. They did not look kindly on resistance from the opposing voices of the Imams. They felt there could be only one true leader in Islam, and so they began the systematic extermination of the dissenting voice controlled by the Imams. From the first Imam, to the eleventh Imam, all were killed on orders from the caliphate. Most of the Imams were poisoned, and one was killed in battle against the caliph and then beheaded.

This led to the widespread oppression of the Shia minority; their Imams were killed by the caliphs and they were never allowed their true voice as expressed by the words of the Imams. The Shia feel that they are a persecuted branch of the Muslim world, and all their hope resides in the coming of an Imam that they feel is destined to rule the world. He is known as the Twelfth Imam. Here is some background information on him.

His father was the eleventh Imam, Hasan al-Askari. He was an Imam that was dominated by the Abbasid caliphate Al-Mu'tamid and was imprisoned in Samarra, Iraq.[23] The Abbasid caliphates were from Iraq and derived their name from the uncle of Muhammad named Abbas. The caliphate kept tight control over the eleventh Imam, so much so that the eleventh Imam sent his son into hiding in order to protect him. He didn't want his son to be controlled by the interference of the caliphate, so his son was secreted away and disappeared from Samarra, Iraq where his father was being held captive by the caliphate.

The one who was secreted away and disappeared is known as the Twelfth Imam. He was born on July 29th, 868 or 869 AD.

---

23 Wikipedia, "Imamah (Shia Doctrine)," http://en.wikipedia.org/wiki/Imamah_(Shia_doctrine).

(Two different dates are given for the year of his birth.)[24] While the one that will be known as the Twelfth Imam was still a young child, he is said to have gone into occultation (hiding), and is due to reappear on the world scene when the time is right for him. He went into occultation (hiding) in 872 AD, and devout Shia Muslims have been awaiting his promised return ever since that time.

The common belief among "Twelvers," those who believe in the return of the Twelfth Imam, (including modern day Iran), is that the Twelfth Imam is going to come out of occultation (hiding) at a time of severe distress among the Islamic people. It will be a time when the Islamic religion has suffered a tremendous defeat, and is the time when world conditions are ideal for his reappearance. It is a time of war and pandemonium reigning on the face of the earth, and the Twelfth Imam is going to emerge to bring peace to the world and order out of chaos.

The long awaited Twelfth Imam has a name; it is Muhammad al-Mahdi. His full name is Muhammad ibn al-Hasan al-Mahdi, but most will know him as Muhammad al-Mahdi or the "Mahdi." He has many titles that he is known by in the Islamic world such as "The Guided One," the "Hidden Imam," "The Proof," the "Lord of our Times," the "One vested with Divine Authority," "God's remainder," and "The one who will rise and fill the universe with Justice."[25] To most of his followers, he will simply be called Mahdi.

Signs of the Return of the Twelfth Imam

In the Islamic world there are many signs given signifying the time is right for his return. What is fascinating, if not a little astounding, is the fact that many of the signs spoken of mirror things that are said in the Bible. Here are some of the signs of the

24 Wikipedia, "Imamah (Shia Doctrine)."
25 Wikipedia, "Imamah (Shia Doctrine)."

imminent return of the Twelfth Imam, given by the Imams themselves, and the correlating evidence that can be found in the Bible.

Words from the Imams	Corresponding areas from the Bible
There will be much conflict throughout the land until Syria is destroyed.	Damascus (in Syria) is going to be destroyed as a city and will be a ruinous heap. (Isaiah 17:1)
Before the one who will arise (Mahdi), there will be red death and white death…as for red death that is from the sword, while white death is from plague.	Rider on the red horse of Revelation 6 signifies war; Rider on the pale horse of Revelation 6 signifies beasts which can also be biological weapons like plague.
The Turk will occupy the region of Al-Jazira. (the area of Northwestern Iraq, Northeastern Syria, and Southeastern Turkey—east of the Euphrates river)	Gog (the Turkish Caliphate) will control the area described after the Psalm 83 war and before his destruction in the Gog/Magog War. (Psalm 83, Ezekiel 38, 39)
A fire will appear for a long time in the east, remaining in the air for three or seven days.	The Lord will send a fire on Magog, and fire will fall from the skies like rain mixed with brimstone. (Ezekiel 39:6, 38: 22)
Abbasids (Iraqis) will be burnt between Jalula and Khaneqin (Two cities northeast of Baghdad near the Iranian border)	Fire will fall on Magog and the bands that are with Gog and other areas in that region. (Ezekiel 39:6)
Earthquake will occur so that much of the city of Baghdad will be swallowed	Great earthquake will occur during the sixth seal of Revelation (Revelation 6:12)
Two signs will arise—there will be an eclipse of the sun in the middle of the month of Ramadan, and an eclipse of the moon at the end of it.	The sun will become black as sackcloth of hair, and the moon became as blood. (Revelation 6:12)

There are many similarities between these accounts. Both speak of Syria being destroyed, both speak of war and death, both speak of fire that will fall from the sky and a great earthquake. Also, in both accounts it mentions things that are going to happen as a sign where blackness envelopes the sun and the moon.

Many of the predictions about the return of the Twelfth Imam have areas in the Bible that correlate precisely with conditions the Imams have described. In fact, what may be surprising to many Christians is the fact that the Imams claim that they have biblical authority for the basis of the Twelve Imams. They base their authority on a Scripture that is found in Genesis. They say that the Bible predicted that there would be twelve princes who would arise and they would be made a great nation. Let's take a look at the Scripture they are referring to.

"And as for Ishmael, I have heard thee: Behold, I have blessed him, and will make him fruitful, and will multiply him exceedingly; *twelve princes shall he beget,* and I will make him a great nation." (Genesis 17: 20)

The Imams and many scholars from the Islamic religion say this is where the Bible gives them authority, because they claim that the "twelve princes" referred to in this Scripture, are in fact the twelve Imams of the Islamic religion. Therefore, they feel that when the Twelfth Imam comes out of hiding, that he will have authority given to him by the Bible over those that believe in the Bible.

Is this really the case?—or are the Islamists twisting God's words and trying to make them say something that was not intended? Whenever we have questions like this, we need to let the Bible interpret the words of the Bible, and not believe someone else's interpretation of what they want the Bible to say. In this example, the Bible is very clear on who the "Twelve Princes" actually are. In Genesis, chapter twenty five, we are told that the twelve princes are the sons of Ishmael—not twelve Imams like the Islamists would like us to believe.

"These are the sons of Ishmael, and these are their names, by their towns, and by their castles; *twelve princes* according to their nations." (Genesis 25:16)

We must always be careful to really understand what the Bible is saying. The Bible will interpret the Bible if you do enough searching and watch for what God is telling you.

One thing that our research shows is that many signs have been given for the return of the Twelfth Imam. Let's also remember the conditions in the world at this point in time. The church has been raptured and is gone from the face of the earth, Gog and his hordes have been defeated in the land of Israel, and the world has experienced a devastating global earthquake. The office of the Caliphate is vacant due to the death of the Turkish Caliphate Gog. The beast empire has suffered a severe head wound with the death of the leader Gog. The world is in turmoil and chaos is rampant due to the devastation of the great earthquake. Islam has suffered their second major defeat. All the conditions are now right for the appearance of the Twelfth Imam. The world stage is set, all it needs now is the appearance of a leader who promises the world everything it wants to hear—but where will he come from?

The Reappearance

Those looking most expectantly for the return of the Mahdi are the leaders in Iran. The people of Iran are primarily Shia (Shiite) Muslims. They are the ones that feel they have been unfairly oppressed at the hands of the Sunni Caliphates. Now that the Turkish Caliphate has been destroyed, they see their opportunity. They have a tradition that their Mahdi is going to return by emerging from a well inside the Jamkaran Mosque in Iran.

This is what the Jamkaran Mosque looks like. Inside this structure is a deep depression that goes down into the earth. This "well" is the place from which the Twelfth Imam is going to re-appear according to Islamic scholars. The Mahdi will somehow rise up out of the earth, and his appearance will be witnessed by many and will send shock waves across the Islamic community. However this happens, someone is going to emerge from the well in Jamkaran, and is going to claim that he is the Twelfth Imam, the long awaited Mahdi.

What is very interesting is how the emergence of the "Mahdi" from deep inside the earth correlates with the appearance of the antichrist in the Book of Revelation. The antichrist comes up out of the earth in a scene that foreshadows something ominous. "And I beheld another beast coming up out of the earth; and he had two horns like a lamb, and he spake as a dragon." (Revelation 13:11) The beast comes up out of the earth—in the exact manner that the Mahdi makes his appearance to the world; rising up from the Jamkaran well in Iran. The correlation between these two appearances is uncanny.

What is even more astounding is that the Book of Revelation further clarifies this event by describing the entity that ascends out of the bottomless pit as being one that had previously lived, and then was not, and yet somehow lives again.

"The beast that thou sawest was and is not; and shall ascend out of the bottomless pit, and go into perdition: and they that dwell on the earth shall wonder, whose names were not written in the book of life from the foundation of the world, when they behold the beast that was, and is not, and yet is." (Revelation 17:8)

I'm not sure how this reappearance is accomplished, but it is quite clear from this Scripture that the antichrist will emerge after having lived previously, and then was gone for a period of time, and yet somehow he is able to emerge on the world stage again. He will rise up out of the earth to take power, and he will have a substantial pedigree to support him. This is made clear in the verses following his reappearance when the description of beast kingdoms is given. Let's take a look at what is said so we can gain some greater understanding.

The Eight Beast Empires

"And there are seven kings; five are fallen, and one is, and the other is not yet come; and when he cometh he must continue a short space. And the beast that was, and is not, even he is the eighth, and is of the seven, and goeth into perdition." (Revelation 17:10-11)

Let's stop here and interpret what has been said. This passage lets us know that there are going to be a total of eight beast empires that will have ruled on earth before Jesus Christ returns again. The antichrist is the ruler of the eighth beast empire, and he is the one that once was, and was not, and yet somehow is, and even more than that he was a part of the seventh beast empire that formerly existed. Who were these beast empires?

At the time this was written by the Apostle John, five beast empires had already been. They were:

1. The Egyptian Empire.
2. The Assyrian Empire.
3. The Babylonian Empire.
4. The Persian Empire.
5. The Greek Empire.

John tells us that one empire "is," and that it is the sixth empire. What empire was in control of the world when the Apostle John wrote these things? The answer to this question is simple. The Roman Empire controlled the Middle East and most of the known world in John's day.

The identification of the seventh beast empire is not as simple as the others—it is the empire that we need to identify. From the clues we are given in this verse, the seventh empire had not yet come in John's day. The Roman Empire was in power in John's day and was the sixth empire. Every other empire preceding the Romans were conquered by the empire coming after them; for example the Egyptians were conquered by the Assyrians, the Assyrians were conquered by the Babylonian...and so on in that manner. Following this pattern, if we really want to know who the seventh empire was, then we need to ask: Who conquered the Roman Empire?

What many people forget is the fact that the Roman Empire split in two in 395 AD, into a western and eastern portion.[26] The western portion of the Roman Empire fell far earlier than the eastern portion. The eastern portion of the Roman Empire continued almost a thousand years after the fall of the western half. It didn't fall until 1453 AD when the Muslim Turks under Mehemet II overran the city of Constantinople. Mehemet II represented the Turkish caliphate of the Islamic empire. His success led to the formation of the Ottoman Empire, a distinctly Muslim empire. The answer to our question about who conquered the Roman Empire is that it was the Islamic Empire under the leadership of the caliphate that accomplished this feat.

---

26 Walid Shoebat, Joel Richardson, *God's War on Terror* (New York, NY: Top Executive Media, 2008), p.302.

Interesting too is the fact that Jerusalem was conquered by an Islamic empire under the direction of the caliph Umar Ibn al-Khattab in 637 AD.

Based on this information then, the seventh beast empire was an Islamic Empire under the direction of the caliphate. This is the beast empire that overthrew Jerusalem and the last vestiges of the Roman Empire in Constantinople.

In light of the identification of the seventh beast empire, an Islamic Empire under the direction of the caliphate, the mystery surrounding the eighth beast empire is more easily understood. The Apostle John said that the eighth beast empire would be "of the seventh." In other words, John is saying that the eighth beast empire would be composed of elements of the seventh beast empire, and would come out of the seventh beast empire. This is more easily recognized now that we understand the background of the Twelfth Imam. He literally went into hiding during the time when the seventh beast empire was in control in 872 AD. He is exactly from the time frame when another caliphate controlled the Islamic empire—so he literally comes out of the seventh beast empire. No other person could possibly fulfill this prediction so precisely and accurately.

When the Twelfth Imam reappears on the scene he will assume leadership of the eighth beast empire as he takes over the office of the caliphate. This fits precisely with his description in Revelation chapter thirteen where it says that the beast will have "two horns like a lamb." (Revelation 13:11) Horns are indicative of leadership, and the antichrist will have two fulfillments of leadership because he will be both the Twelfth Imam, and he will be the leader of the caliphate. The two horns represent the office of the Twelfth Imam and the office of the caliphate. As such, he will be the undisputed leader of the Islamic world.

This fits precisely with what is said in Revelation where it says the beast will be, and then will not be, and then will be again. (Revelation 17:8) Both the office of the Twelfth Imam and the office of the caliphate have suffered that exact fate. There had been eleven previous Imams functioning in that office until they died, and then the Twelfth Imam went into occultation in the year 872 AD to preserve his life. The office of the caliphate was formed after the death of Muhammad and was in existence for centuries until March 3rd, 1924 when it was disbanded. It wasn't until recently that the office of the caliphate was brought back into being on June 29th, 2014. The leadership office of the Twelfth Imam will be present again when the Mahdi comes out of hiding—so in that way, the two leadership roles of the eighth beast empire will have been, and then were no longer, but are yet again in the world. Both will be functioning again when the Mahdi rises to power.

The antichrist, the Mahdi and the Twelfth Imam are all the same person and he is the leader of the eighth beast empire. He is part of the seventh beast empire because he came directly out of it. The seventh beast empire was the Islamic Empire under the direction of the caliphate. The eighth beast empire is an Islamic Empire with the antichrist holding two leadership roles, the Twelfth Imam and the office of the caliphate.

Now we can complete our list of the eight beast empires.

6. The Roman Empire.

7. The Islamic Empire under the direction of the caliphate which became the Ottoman Empire.

8. The Islamic Empire under the direction of the Twelfth Imam and caliphate (the two horns) and manifested in the antichrist.

The Pedigree of the Antichrist

The antichrist will have the pedigree to stake his claim as ruler of all of Islam. He will be an Assyrian because his father came from an area that used to be part of the Assyrian empire, Iraq. This is important because in many places in the Bible, the Assyrian is synonymous with the antichrist. (See Isaiah 10:24, 14:25, 30:31, 31:8) He will also be the Twelfth Imam because he fulfills all the prophecies of the long awaited Mahdi and will claim that he is the hidden Imam. And he will claim the vacated office of the caliphate, saying it belongs to him—thus uniting the office of the caliphate and the office of the Imam. It will be the first time in over a thousand years that this has happened.

The antichrist will move quickly to consolidate his power. His charm and overall appeal will allow him to attain celebrity status very quickly. When some rise up to oppose him, he will overthrow any that stand in his way on his path to power. The Bible says that three leaders will stand in his way and be overthrown. (Daniel 7:25)

The antichrist will have the house of Israel in his sights and will convince many in Israel that he is their long awaited Messiah. He will be able to do this by convincing the multitudes that the destruction of Gog and his forces was the battle of Armageddon; and that it is now time for their Messiah to come and usher in a time of peace. He will claim that he is their promised Savior, and that there is going to be peace in their time. He will promise that he has all the answers to ensure peace, but Israel will have to sign a peace agreement with him in order for peace to take place. Many in Israel will be misled, and will enthusiastically sign the peace agreement, which the Scriptures call "the covenant with death." (Isaiah 28:18)

At the exact moment the peace deal is signed with the antichrist, the final seven year period of time, the 70th week of Daniel, begins. (Daniel 9:27) The Lord's clock starts counting down once again.

Those in the house of Israel that were sealed for the service of the Lord (the 144,000) will not be deceived by the promises of the antichrist. They will be an impediment to his agenda, and will actively oppose him. The Scriptures say that "the people that do know their God shall be strong, and do exploits. And they that understand among the people shall instruct many." (Daniel 11:32-33)

The people of Israel are going to need all the help they can get because once the antichrist appears; he will go on a rampage that only God can stop.

Chapter Twenty One

THE EXPLOITS OF THE ANTICHRIST

When the antichrist arrives on the world scene, we have entered a totally new era in the history of mankind. Almost everything that we are familiar with in the world will no longer apply.

For example, the Day of the Lord will have begun, and as we have already discussed, the Day of the Lord issues in a period of great destruction on the earth. The world will still be reeling from the destructive events when the great earthquake struck. It will take a substantial period of time to get the electrical grid functioning again. And getting the cities livable again will be a monumental task. Transportation will be hampered until the roads are made passable again. The world will be a living nightmare that will only get worse over time until the Lord comes again.

When you include the fact that followers of Christ will have been raptured, then you add an unknown dimension to the world situation. The ones who have: looked out for the welfare and good of others, have placed others first over their own needs, have consistently demonstrated an attitude of love towards others, have been the backbone of their communities and done the tasks that no one else wanted to do, and have made the world a better place by their love and service to others are going to be gone. The Lord has taken them to be with Him—and the world will feel a terrible void in their absence.

This is one of the reasons the world will find the antichrist so attractive. He will promise to fill the void in the lives of so many people on the earth. But this will be a promise that he is unable to keep. His true nature will rise to the forefront, and soon he will not be able to stop himself from demonstrating his contempt for any that will not bend to the force of his will. He will not tolerate any that oppose him, and will actively move to suppress their opinions and their voice. He will quickly set himself up to be the ruler of the world and he will stop at nothing to usurp the throne that is reserved for Jesus Christ.

We have not been left uninformed about how the antichrist arises and the way that he achieves his pathway to power. God's Word is full of references about him, in fact there are more references about the last days and conditions in the world during his reign of power than there are about Jesus Christ's first coming to the world. We need to review some of those references so we can understand more about him.

Scriptures Referencing the Antichrist

1. He comes up out of the earth (Revelation 13:11), out of the bottomless pit. (Revelation 17:8)
2. He rises to power through the occult, and uses the power of the occult to achieve his desires. (Daniel 8:23-25)

There needs to be a point of clarification on this point. The antichrist was hidden through a process known as "occultation." This is some form of secret and esoteric ritual involving the black arts which hides a person until the time of their revealing. Another ritualistic black arts ceremony is required to bring the person out of hiding for their unveiling to the world. The antichrist will emerge following just such a ritual. The conclusion we can draw from this information is that the antichrist was hidden and will arise from some sort of satanic ritualistic process. This is exactly what the Scripture in Daniel is telling us. "A king of fierce countenance, and understanding dark sentences, shall stand up." (Daniel 8:23) In other words, the antichrist will have understanding of black magic, and will come to power through the occult.

Daniel also tells us that he will have incredible power supporting him, but it will not come through him—he will tap into the power of satanic sources. "And his power shall be mighty, but not by his own power." (Daniel 8:24) The antichrist will be so comfortable with the satanic power at his disposal that he will encourage people to get involved with black magic, and indulge in the satanic arts. "And through his policy also he shall cause craft to prosper in his hand." (Daniel 8:25) One thing is certain during the reign of the antichrist—black magic and satanic rituals will become routine and commonplace while he is in power.

3. The antichrist overthrows three kings in order to come to power. He will need to overthrow three rulers in positions of power to rise to the point where he can solidify his world dominion. (Daniel 7:8)

4. He heals the deadly head wound of the beast empire. (Revelation 13:3) He does this by restoring the office of the Imam after it had been gone for a significant period

of time and revives the office of the caliphate. He is literally the Twelfth Imam.

5. He signs a peace treaty with Israel that he says will guarantee the nation of Israel peace in their time. (Daniel 9:27) This act initiates the 70th week of Daniel, the final seven year period of time before Jesus returns to set up His kingdom in the world.

6. He will deceive and destroy many by the peace treaty he sets up. (Daniel 8:25) This peace treaty will allow him to do as he wishes, and by his peaceful deceit he will be able to destroy whomever he chooses, in order to perpetuate the illusion of peace.

7. He will set up world dominion. He wants to rule the world, and he will be able to achieve this goal. The Bible says that "Power was given him over all kindreds, and tongues, and nations." (Revelation 13:7)

8. To demonstrate his power and control over the world, he will cause all to receive a mark of his beast empire. (Revelation 13:16)

This point needs some further clarification also. The mark that people receive will be in their right hand or in their forehead, and will in some way be a representation of the beast kingdom from which he arose. The antichrist will use this identification mark as some sort of control for regulating everything that you need in life to survive. People will not be able to buy anything such as food or basic goods without using this mark. In this way the antichrist will have power over all people, and will probably receive some revenue stream whenever this mark is employed. One thing we need to realize is that the antichrist is the Twelfth Imam, and the eleven Imams before him all had marks or symbols that signified their power. It is perfectly normal for this Twelfth Imam to demand that all of his followers be identified by his mark or symbol also. Here is a representation of what the mark or symbol of the Twelfth Imam may look like:

Somehow, the symbol the antichrist uses is associated with the number 666. A stylized rendition of this mark will be used to identify his followers and facilitate their ability to procure goods and services, and will be imprinted or imbedded on the right hands or foreheads of his acolytes. The Bible describes this in the following way: "And he causeth all, both small and great, rich and poor, free and bond, to receive a mark in their right hand, or in their foreheads: and that no man might buy or sell, save he that had the mark, or the name of the beast, or the number of his name. Here is wisdom. Let him that hath understanding count the number of the beast: for it is the number of a man; and his number is Six hundred threescore and six." (Revelation 13:16-18)

John the Apostle warns us that no person should ever receive the mark of the beast. If you do, you will be subject to the wrath of God that will be poured out in the bowl and trumpet judgments and you will be separated from God forever. (Revelation 14:9-11)

9. He will wage war against the saints, and will overcome them. (Revelation 13:7)

Where do these saints come from and why is he able to overcome them? Not all of the people in the churches are going to be protected by the rapture. There are simply too many people in churches today who do not listen to what Jesus has said to them. They do whatever they feel is right in their own eyes. They have no idea that the Bible actually says, and have no relationship with Jesus Christ because they have never taken the time to get to know Him. They justify their actions by an irrational set of rules that neither justifies nor protects them when the destructive events associated with the Day of the Lord come upon them. Consequently they have missed the rapture and are described as being unwise, lukewarm, and those that will be thrown into the great tribulation. In the letters to the seven churches, many are characterized in this manner, and numerous warnings are given to them to change their ways or face the consequences of great tribulation when they are left behind after the rapture. No doubt these people who have some knowledge of the Bible will realize their error after the rapture has occurred. Only then will they recognize they didn't really know the Lord and will finally turn to Him. The saints being referenced in this Scripture are the ones that fall into this category, and while they are trying to change their ways and follow Jesus as best they can in their new circumstances; they will find it extremely difficult and many will be overcome by the antichrist's wanton destruction of Christians and Jews. This is the same fate that was shared by the Jewish people after their rejection of Jesus Christ during the diaspora. They suffered unspeakable horrors and a holocaust because of their refusal to follow their Messiah.

10. The antichrist will change times and laws. (Daniel 7:25)

This is another reference that makes no sense until we realize what has happened just prior to the antichrist arriving on the world scene. When the destruction associated with the Day of the Lord begins, a great earthquake is going to shake the entire world. This earthquake is going to be so severe that "the earth shall remove out of her place." (Isaiah 13:13) This means that the orbit of the earth is going to be disrupted. There are numerous sources that have stated that the earth moving out of its stationary orbit in the past has been caused by the earth interacting with a planet-sized body in a cosmic close encounter. A good example is Donald Wesley Patten's book, *Catastrophism and the Old Testament*, or the works by Immanuel Velikovsky such as *World's in Collision* or *Earth in Upheaval*.

When a planet-sized interstellar body comes close enough to the earth, we would have the exact effects described in Ezekiel 38 and 39, and the Day of the Lord judgments including a global earthquake and sheets of fire falling out of the skies. This would explain how our planet could be moved out of orbit also, since the gravitational pull of the passing body could shorten our orbit until it resembled the orbit the earth used to have in ancient days. In the book *Catastrophism and the Old Testament*, Donald Patten cites that every ancient culture had years that were 360 days in length. This includes Arabia, Assyria, Babylonia, China, Egypt, Greece, India, Japan, Mexico, Palestine, Persia, Peru and early Rome. Every one of these cultures had years that were 360 days. This is the basis for 360 degrees in a circle. As a consequence of the earthquake and cosmic encounter which will shorten the orbit of the earth, the antichrist will need to change time to accurately reflect the true period of the year which will change to 360 days a year.

Another place that verifies the earth's new orbit will be 360 days a year is found in the book of Daniel. Daniel tells us that the time at which the antichrist enters the Jewish temple, stops the daily sacrifice, and desecrates the Jewish temple is going to be the midpoint of the final seven year period of time, or three and a half years into the seven year period. Revelation then specifies the number of days that will be—and it says that it is exactly 1260 days. (Revelation 12:6) The only way three and a half years totals 1260 days is by having a calendar year of 360 days, not the current 365¼ days a year we have now. (See Revelation 12:6 and Daniel 9:27) Therefore, sometime before the appearance of the antichrist, earth's orbit is going to be shortened to 360 days a year.

The antichrist is also going to change laws by instituting Sharia Law in the areas he controls. Sharia Law is the moral code and religious law of the Islamic religion. It is characterized by harsh punishments such as flogging, stoning, and the cutting off of one's hands for more serious infractions. This is strictly an Islamic law, and reinforces the fact that the antichrist is going to be from the Islamic religion.

11. The antichrist shall not regard the God of his fathers, nor the desire of women. (Daniel 11:37)

This is another point that needs further clarification. Many have said that the fact the antichrist does not regard the desire of women means that he is homosexual. When we closely examine this Scripture, a more accurate interpretation may mean that women have such insignificant standing in the hierarchy of the antichrist's religion that he doesn't care what they want or desire. The Islamic culture is centered around men, with the desires of women being a secondary concern. In this way, the antichrist does not regard the desire of women.

The fact that the antichrist does not regard the God of his fathers should be disturbing to those in the Muslim religion. This probably means that the antichrist is not driven by the teachings of Islam as much as he is driven to use all means at his disposal to accomplish his goals. It says that he will "Honor the god of forces" (Daniel 11:38) and that he shall acknowledge a "strange god." (Daniel 11:39) What is meant by a "strange god?" If we combine what these two Scriptures are saying then we can conclude that some sort of strange god is going to appear that somehow has control of the forces around him. Is this referring to some sort of "alien deception?" Is the antichrist going to rise to power on the heels of some sort of alien disclosure that will shock the world into believing in some foreign alien god?

We already know that the antichrist arises to take power through some sort of ritual of the occult. This ritual will be satanic in nature, and we know that satanic forces use deception as a common means to accomplish their purposes. The minions of Satan could be posing as an alien presence to orchestrate a grand delusion that casts doubt on the religious history of the world. The antichrist, being the opportunist that he is, will use the deceptive masquerade of the alien presence to cement and consolidate his rise to power, and in that way will fulfill the Scripture where it says he will not regard the God of his fathers (Daniel 11:37) but will acknowledge a strange god that is a god of forces. Two books have proposed this theory. They are *Alien Encounters* by Chuck Missler and Mark Eastman, and *Exo-Vaticana* by Cris Putnam and Thomas Horn. Both books provide excellent documentation to support this theory of alien deception and I would encourage you to read them if you would like more information on this subject.

12. The antichrist will be a great deceiver.
    (2 Thessalonians 2:11)

13. He will show signs and lying wonders.
    (2 Thessalonians 2:9) This can be accomplished
    by the assistance of occultic forces—or by the

assistance of a deceptive alien presence which is really satanic powers manifesting a great delusion.

14. He will cause fire to come down from heaven. (Revelation 13:13)

This point must be commented upon. One of the things that the Lord will do to protect the nation of Israel when the armies of Gog are arrayed against them is to cause fire to fall from heaven to destroy the coalition of Magog. The rain of fire from heaven is a method that the Lord uses to protect His people. The antichrist will be claiming that he is God, and so it is natural that he will try to mimic the power of God by doing something that God has done. He will be able to cause fire to come down from heaven by the power of the satanic forces at his disposal. Satan is always trying to mimic things the Lord has done and because the antichrist is an agent of Satan, he will have the ability to make fire come down from heaven also.

15. The antichrist will have the ability to give life to inanimate objects. (Revelation 13:15)

What in the world does this mean? How is it possible to give life to inanimate objects? Before we comment on this, let's review what the Scripture has to say. "And he had power to give life unto the image of the beast, that the image of the beast should both speak, and cause that as many as would not worship the image of the beast should be killed." (Revelation 13:15) This is a clear reference to the application of artificial intelligence, and can be the result of design or demonic possession. People are going to be making images (idols), and then these images are going to have artificial intelligence capabilities placed within them that are demonic in nature. This is clear because when the images speak, they are going to say that people should be killed if they are not worshipping the demonically imbued idols that represent the antichrist. This will be a way that the antichrist will be able to exert control over the world and will enable him to discover all those that are not worshipping him.

16. He will set himself up to be worshipped as God in the Jewish temple. (2 Thessalonians 2:4)

This is one of the milestone events that occur in the life of the antichrist. Three and a half years into the seven year period that fulfills Israel's destiny (Daniel 9:27), the antichrist is going to enter the Jewish temple. This means that the Jewish Temple will be rebuilt sometime before the antichrist arrives on the world scene. He will proceed into the Holy of Holies, a place reserved for God, and will set himself up to be worshiped as God. This act is going to be known as the abomination of desolation, or the abomination that makes desolate. No one is ever to be in the Holy of Holies in the Jewish temple except the high priest on one day in the year. This is a place reserved for God. The fact that the antichrist enters it is a desecration of the Jewish temple. God looks on this as an abomination. The antichrist wants to be worshipped by the entire world as God, and entering and setting himself up to be worshipped in the Jewish temple is a natural way for him to make that proclamation.

This act allows many in the house of Israel who have been misled to see the antichrist for who he really is—a great deceiver. When those in Israel realize his true identity, some will escape from the city of Jerusalem as the antichrist's forces move to seal off the city. They will flee to a place where God will protect them (Isaiah 26:20) while the Lord unleashes a great destruction upon the whole earth. (Isaiah 28:22) The Lord's anger (Isaiah 26:20) is consistent with the trumpet and vial judgments we see described in Revelation.

17. Following the trumpet and vial judgments, as his final act of defiance, the antichrist will lead the remaining forces in the world into the Battle of Armageddon. (Revelation 16:16)

18. The antichrist will be cast alive into the lake of fire and brimstone after his armies are defeated in the Battle of Armageddon. (Revelation 19:20)

The antichrist is going to meet his fate when he comes against Jesus Christ, who will return to the earth at His second coming. The antichrist's brief career as ruler of the world will be brought to an end when the rightful heir of the world comes to take the throne that He paid for with His own blood.

The scene on the earth will be unlike anything anyone can imagine, and when Armageddon takes place, few will realize that this battle fulfills a biblical precedent just like the Psalm 83 War and the Gog/Magog War. Only this time the house of Israel will not reject their Messiah as they have done in times past. Instead, they will join in the call for Jesus to lead their forces and as a nation will call for the return of their Savior. All voices in Israel will be saying, "Blessed is he that cometh in the name of the Lord." (Matthew 23:39) This is the fulfillment of prophesy that the Lord says will have to happen before He will physically return to the earth again.

The Lord will hear the voice of His people from Heaven, and will answer their call.

Chapter Twenty Two

THE THIRD WAR IN ISRAEL'S FUTURE, THE BATTLE OF ARMAGEDDON

After a seven year reign of terror on the earth, the antichrist is going to meet (more than) his match when Jesus Christ returns to the earth to assume the throne that He had paid for with His own blood. What will the condition of the world be like before this time?

The world is going to be ravaged by the sheer number of destructive events that are going to happen as the Day of the Lord ensues. Everything prior to this is merely a prelude to the destruction that is going to be unleashed on the earth after the Day of the Lord commences.

The Book of Revelation gives us a terrifying description of the fate the world after the destructive events begin. We are told that hail and fire mingled with blood are going to be falling out of the sky and because of this phenomenon one third of the trees are going to be burnt up. "The first angel sounded, and there followed hail and fire mingled with blood, and they were cast upon the earth: and the third part of trees was burnt up, and all green grass was burnt up." (Revelation 8:7)

A huge mountain like object is going to enter the earth's atmosphere and become engulfed in fire, and then plunge into the depths of the seas. This event is going to be so destructive that one third of all the life in the sea is going to die, and one third of all the ships on the ocean are going to be destroyed. "And the second angel sounded, and as it were a great mountain burning with fire was cast into the sea: and the third part of the sea became blood; and the third part of the creatures which were in the sea, and had life, died, and the third part of the ships were destroyed." (Revelation 8:8-9)

When the third trumpet sounds, a great star burning as a lamp is going to fall upon the waters of the world, polluting the waters of the world and making them bitter. Because the waters of the world are going to be polluted, many people are going to die. "And the third angel sounded, and there fell a great star from heaven, burning as it were a lamp, and it fell upon the third part of the rivers, and upon the fountains of waters; and the name of the star is call Wormwood: and the third part of the waters became wormwood; and many men died of the waters, because they were made bitter." (Revelation 8:10-11)

The destructive events continue and because of the catastrophic events such as the great mountain falling into the ocean and fire falling from heaven, the atmosphere of the earth is going to become polluted so that the sun the moon and the stars are going to be obscured for a third part of the day and night. "And the fourth angel sounded, and the third part of the sun was smitten, and the third part of the moon, and the third part of the stars; so as the third part of them was darkened, and the day shone not for a third part of it, and the night likewise." (Revelation 8:12)

As disturbing as these descriptions may sound, they are not the worst of the things that are going to be released upon the earth. The Book of Revelation next describes three woes that are going to be unleashed from their confinement to wreak havoc upon the world. They are all demonic forces and they are going to cause untold terror and destruction in the world.

The first of the demonic forces is a king from the bottomless pit known as Abaddon or Apollyon. He brings a multitude of demonic forces with him shaped like locusts that have the power to torment men for five months. The demonic locusts have scorpion like tails with which they sting and hurt people. (Revelation 9:1-11)

The second woe involves the releasing of four fallen angels which were bound in the Euphrates River. When they are freed from their captivity, they will lead an army of two hundred million. This massive army will destroy one third of the people left in the world by the fire, smoke and brimstone they release upon the people of the world. (Revelation 9:14-21)

The third and final woe is when the devil is cast out of heaven down to the earth. (Revelation 12:12) When Satan is cast out of heaven he is going to have great wrath and will persecute the house of Israel and the remnant of the saints that are left on the earth. These are the saints that were not diligent at the time of the rapture, but have since kept the commandments of God and now have the testimony of Jesus Christ.

People are going to be astounded by the things that have been released upon the earth during the trumpet judgments. Men's hearts are going to melt with fear when they see the things that are coming on the earth because of the judgment of God. Natural disasters will be inundating the earth, and demonic forces will be running rampant across the face of the world. These demonic forces will be so terrifying that people's hearts will be failing when they see them. The Book of Luke describes the destructive events that begin with the Day of the Lord in the following way:

"And there shall be signs in the sun, and in the moon, and in the stars: and upon the earth distress of nations, with perplexity; and sea and the waves roaring. Men's hearts failing them for fear, and for looking after those things which are coming on the earth: for the powers of heaven shall be shaken." (Luke 21:25-26)

The Two Witnesses

This will truly be a terrible time to live on the earth. The only ones standing in the way of the antichrist and the demonic hordes that have been unleashed in the world are the 144,000 special witnesses of Christ that were set apart for service to God in the twelve tribes of Israel, and the two witnesses we see described in the eleventh chapter of Revelation. These two special witnesses will have the power to stop the rain, turn the waters to blood, and cause plagues to come upon the earth. They will have the power to protect themselves, and will prophesy on the earth for 1260 days. (Revelation 11:3-6)

When the two witnesses have finished their testimony, the antichrist will be allowed to kill them, and their dead bodies will lie where they fell for three-and-a-half days, unburied. At the end of three-and-a-half days, the two witnesses shall stand on their feet again, and will ascend into heaven when the Lord calls them to "Come up hither." (Revelation 11:7-12)

The two witnesses and the 144,000 will have been such a thorn in the side of the antichrist that he eventually decides to destroy all the house of Israel. He is going to disregard the peace treaty he signed with them, and will call for all the armies that are left in the world to gather on the plains of Megiddo, to prepare to completely annihilate all the covenant people of Israel.

The kings of the world and their armies are deceived by the antichrist and the demonic forces in the world working miracles to get them to come to Armageddon. "For they are the spirits of devils, working miracles, which go forth unto the kings of the earth and of the whole world, to gather them to the battle of that great day of God Almighty. And He gathered them together into a place called in the Hebrew tongue Armageddon." (Revelation 16:14, 16)

The Third War in the Biblical Precedent

The battle of Armageddon is the third war in the biblical precedent, the third war in which the house of Israel fulfills its prophetic destiny. In ancient times, Nebuchadnezzar destroyed the nation of Israel and led its people into captivity in the third war. This time, when the antichrist comes against them, the house of Israel is going to be successful in this third war, and will do something that they have never done before in modern times. They are going to acknowledge their offense against their Messiah, and every person in Israel is going to say, "Blessed is he that cometh in the name of the Lord." (Matthew 23:39)

These words set the stage for the return of Jesus Christ as he comes once again to His people. The house of Israel is no longer going to reject their Savior, but will ask for Him to return to them. This time the house of Israel will be protected; they will fulfill their prophetic destiny and will triumph over the forces of the antichrist because Jesus Christ leads His armies in triumph over the forces of evil.

The antichrist will not know what hit him. As he and the armies of the world prepare to attack Israel, they will be overwhelmed by Jesus Christ leading the armies of the Lord. Armageddon will not be much of a war because the armies of the antichrist will be destroyed almost immediately by the forces that the Lord brings against them.

Not only will Jesus be leading an army sitting on white horses and clothed in white linen, (Revelation 19:14) but He will cause the greatest earthquake to ever hit the world to occur at the same time. This earthquake will be so large that every island in the ocean to going to flee away, and the mountains are no longer going to be found. "And there was a great earthquake, such as was not since men were upon the earth, so mighty an earthquake, and so great...And every island fled away, and the mountains were not found." (Revelation 16:18, 20)

This is not the only natural disaster that will occur at the time of Armageddon. A plague of hail stones will fall out of the sky on people, each one weighing about a talent. (A talent is said to weigh between 75 to 110 pounds in today's measurements.) This plague of hail stones falling from the sky will fall on men who have blasphemed God, and the plague will be very great. "And there fell upon men a great hail out of heaven, every stone about the weight of a talent: and men blasphemed God because of the plague of the hail; for the plague thereof was exceeding great." (Revelation 16:21)

The armies of the antichrist will be destroyed when the Lord returns. The antichrist will be thrown alive into a lake of fire and brimstone along with the false prophet that preformed miracles. Thus ends the horrific career of the most diabolical man to ever walk the face of the earth.

The Three Wars as a Biblical Precedent

The conclusion of the battle of Armageddon ends the three war precedent pattern found in the Bible. The nation of Israel will be the people of the Lord from this point on, and He will be their God. They will have been protected as a nation in each circumstance where their enemies have threatened them. Let's summarize how the modern day wars that will be fought in Israel mirror the wars that took place when Israel was destroyed as a nation in ancient times.

Ancient Biblical Pattern War	Modern Day War in Israel
In 722 BC, ten of the tribes of Israel were carried into captivity when Sargon II finished the siege and destruction of Samaria. This was the first war that began the breakup of Israel as a nation in their land. This led to the loss and the control of lands that had been in their possession from the time of Kind David to King Solomon.	Sometime following the last blood moon of September 28th, 2015, the nation of Israel will be attacked by the Psalm 83 coalition of nations. Israel will be protected by the IDF using nuclear weapons. The victory in this war will lead to the control of lands that the ten tribes formerly controlled and will include lands that God has said is theirs from the Nile river to the Euphrates River.
In 701 BC, the Assyrians under Sennacherib brought an army of 185,000 men and laid siege to the city of Jerusalem. Sennacherib's army was destroyed in one night by heavenly intervention by an angel of the Lord because the Jewish people repented and turned to the Lord for help.	Gog, a Turkish caliph, will lead a coalition of nations known as Magog that will launch a surprise attack on the nation of Israel. The Lord will use heavenly intervention to destroy the forces of Gog and Magog. Gog will die and be buried on the plains of Israel, and only one sixth of his army will escape destruction.
In 586 BC, the Babylonian Ruler Nebuchadnezzar laid siege to the city of Jerusalem and defeated the Jewish people. The city of Jerusalem was destroyed and the Jewish people were carried off into captivity. The Jewish people and the house of Israel failed to achieve their prophetic destiny and were dispersed throughout the world.	The antichrist combines the office of the Twelfth Imam and the caliphate together and gathers the armies of the world together at Armageddon to destroy the house of Israel. Jesus Christ returns to Israel leading the armies of the Lord and defeats the antichrist and his forces. The house of Israel fulfills its prophetic destiny and Jesus Christ sits on the Throne of God in Jerusalem.

This concludes the three wars that set the biblical precedent for the future wars in Israel. What is interesting to note is that there are several things that set a pattern in our study of these events. For example, the blood moon tetrad appearing in the past for Israel during 1949/1950, and again in 1967/1968, set a pattern during which the nation of Israel was at war and gained land that was granted to them by God. It is my conclusion that this pattern will hold true during the blood moon tetrad of 2014/2015. Consequently, soon after the final blood moon appears on September 28th, 2015, Israel will be involved in another war fighting for its survival. They will be victorious in this war just as they have been in 1948 and 1967 and as a result they will have all the land set aside for them by the Lord in Genesis. This war leads to the Gog/Magog war and eventually to the battle of Armageddon.

What is equally surprising to me are the events surrounding the Day of the Lord. The Day of the Lord starts with a war (Gog/Magog) and ends with a war (Armageddon). It begins with a great earthquake, and ends with the greatest earthquake to ever strike the earth. It starts with the Transcendent Event, and it ends with the Second Coming of Jesus Christ. Before the Day of the Lord starts, the church is protected, and before it ends the house of Israel is protected and reunited with their Messiah.

In the end, the house of Israel emerges victorious and takes their rightful position in the world. The raptured church returns to the earth when the Lord returns and is forever with the Lord.

If you noticed in the writing of this book, I always referred to those who would be raptured as being wise. Why did I use that terminology as a distinction for those who will be raptured?

The answer to that question is that I was specifically prompted to use the word "wise" when referring to the Christians that will be raptured. The reason for this, I explain in the next chapter.

Chapter Twenty Three

A WARNING TO THE CHURCH

Why do I refer to the raptured church as being "wise?" Is this some terminology that was invented for convenience sake, or was this term used for a specific purpose?

What does it mean to be "wise" in the eyes of the Lord? Are we given any examples in the Scriptures?

There is a place in God's Word where we are told precisely what God meant when he counseled us to be wise. It is found in the Gospel of Matthew in a parable speaking of the Ten Virgins. Let's take a look at this parable so we can understand exactly what the Lord is telling us.

The Parable of the Ten Virgins

"Then shall the kingdom of heaven be likened unto ten virgins, which took their lamps and went forth to meet the bridegroom." (Matthew 25:1)

Let's stop here and do an analysis on what has just been said. First, what does the term "virgin" mean? The reference to virgins in this parable is in the spiritual sense—in other words they have not worshipped any other God than Jesus Christ. Jesus is their Lord, and Him only have they worshipped. In essence, they are spiritually pure and have not been distracted into focusing their time and attention on the myriad other things vying for our attention. Our Lord has made it quite clear that worshipping any other god is one of the most glaring offenses against Him. This is referred to as spiritual fornication, and there are many references in God's Word where it is condemned (Ezekiel 6:9, Isaiah 26:13, Isaiah 42:17). These virgins, we can conclude, are spiritually pure and have only worshipped Jesus Christ.

Another term we need to define is "lamps." What do lamps refer to in this parable? The lamps have a deeper meaning than something that just provides light. If we look at the Scriptures to interpret the meaning of the lamps we find the following. In Psalms 119:105 we are told "Thy word is a lamp unto my feet, and a light unto my path." Therefore, the deeper implication is that the lamps represent the Word of God. Being familiar with the Word of God represented by His Scriptures is critical for any believer. We absolutely need to know what God has said in the Bible. If we do, then God's Word will be a lamp in our lives and light the way in times of darkness.

The bridegroom in this parable is Jesus Christ. This is made clear in Revelation 19:7-9 where it speaks of the marriage of the Lamb. The marriage supper of the Lamb is prepared for Christ's church and for his saints. It says in Revelation, "Blessed are they which are called unto the marriage supper of the Lamb." (Revelation 19:9) For the wise virgins, this is going to be an event that brings true blessings in their lives.

Let's continue on with the parable: "And five of them were wise, and five were foolish. They that were foolish took their lamps, and took no oil with them: But the wise took oil in their lamps." (Matthew 25:2)

What constitutes being wise in the eyes of the Lord? True wisdom and being wise is defined precisely in Matthew.

"Therefore everyone who hears these words of mine and puts them into practice is like a wise man who built his house on a rock." (Matthew 7:24 NIV)

This means that being wise consists of two things: Hearing the sayings of the Lord and then doing them. How do we hear the sayings of the Lord? The only way we can do that is by reading and studying the Bible. This is a real problem in the church today. Countless surveys have shown that over fifty per cent of today's church members don't ever read the Bible. They don't know what God's Word says because they never read it. When you don't read the Bible, you are missing out on the guidance and direction of the Holy Spirit, which is represented by the oil in the lamps.

In other words, the wise are those who read the Word of God and hear what the Lord is telling them, and then actually do the things they are told in the Bible. Because they are doing this, they have the guidance and direction of the Holy Spirit, the oil in their lamps.

Likewise, being foolish is also defined in the Scriptures. "But everyone who hears these words of mine and does not put them into practice is like a foolish man who built his house on sand. The rain came down, the streams rose, and the winds blew and beat against that house, and it fell with a great crash." (Matthew 7:26-27 NIV)

Someone who is foolish hears the Word of God, but then does not put into practice anything that they have heard. If we constantly ignore what the Scriptures are telling us, then we negate the guidance and direction the Holy Spirit is giving us—in essence there is no oil in our lamps.

We have become the most scripturally illiterate generation ever to live. When prayer and Bible reading were outlawed in our schools on June 17th, 1963, in the *Abington vs. Schempp* Supreme Court decision[27] we started on a path where young people stopped reading the Bible in schools and stopped the routine study of all of God's concepts in His Word. When we don't study the Bible when we are young, we rarely pick up the habit later in life. This has led to the situation we find ourselves in today. The vast majority of people in our churches simply do not read the Bible, and because of this negligence they are missing out on the guidance and direction the Holy Spirit gives us as we read God's Word.

Many who call themselves Christians today live by a dangerous brand of Christianity where they simply do what is right in their own eyes. They don't really know what God's Word says and so they make up their own brand of Christianity that is an amalgamated mess of different philosophies. They have compromised with the teachings of the world so much that they are not a true follower of Jesus Christ and stand on very shaky ground. They are in danger of missing the rapture.

This is the focus of the rest of the Parable of the Ten Virgins. The wise virgins were ready for Jesus Christ when He sent to have them gathered up. They went with Him where they will be protected in heaven during the rapture. The foolish virgins will find

---

27 Bruce J Dierenfield, "The Most Hated Woman in America: Madalyn Murray and the Crusade Against School Prayer", Journal of Supreme Court History 32, no. 1 (2007) pp. 62-84

themselves shut out and will miss the rapture (the reference of the door being shut). Here's what the rest of the parable says:

"And while they went to buy, the bridegroom came; and they that were ready went in with him to the marriage: and the door was shut. Afterward came also the other virgins, saying, Lord, Lord, open to us. But he answered and said, Verily I say unto you, I know you not." (Matthew 25:10-12)

These are probably some of the most frightening words someone who calls themselves a Christian can ever hear—when the Lord says, I know you not. How can this be? The foolish virgins have said that they are Christians after all—they haven't worshipped any other god, and they say that they believe in Jesus Christ...so how can they be shut out during the rapture?

The answer to this question is found earlier in the Gospel of Matthew. In fact, the exact same phrase the foolish virgins use is repeated exactly—Lord, Lord. Let's look at why the Lord said they were shut out from His presence.

"Not everyone that saith unto me, Lord, Lord, shall enter into the kingdom of heaven; but he that doeth the will of my Father which is in heaven. Many will say to me in that day, Lord, Lord, have we not prophesied in thy name? And in thy name have cast out devils: and in thy name done many wonderful works? And then will I profess unto them, I never knew you: depart from me, ye that work iniquity." (Matthew 7:21-23)

The logical question here is: How can people who are doing things "in Jesus' name" not belong to Him?

The answer is right there in the verse. Jesus said He "never knew them"...in other words, Jesus had no relationship with them. These people hadn't taken the time to get know Jesus, had failed to read about Him in His Word, had never tried to understand what He said, and had never talked to Him through prayer. In essence, they had no relationship with Jesus Christ. He doesn't know them at all. The things they were doing were glorifying themselves; Jesus had no part in their attempts at good works.

If what I have just pointed out describes you in any way, then you need to **stop** what you are doing right now, and immediately **begin to talk to God through prayer. Change what you are doing in your life that is alienating you from the Lord**, and resolve to **begin reading the Bible** and begin **doing** the things that He tells you in His Word. Don't continue living your life as you always have but change and become closer to God. If you ask for the Lord's help, He is faithful and will always help you.

One of the worst disasters awaiting a person is to miss the rapture and be shut out from the Lord's presence. Resolve to never let that happen to you.

If you think that you can wait to change until you see some of the events of this book start to happen, then you are playing with fire. The great earthquake that initiates the Day of the Lord destructions is unpredictable, and if you find yourself caught up in the great earthquake, then you have waited too long. God will already have taken His followers home to be with Him, and you will have to face the most hellish conditions that will ever come upon the earth.

I don't know the date of the rapture—that is totally up to God. He is the one who knows when the timing is right. You need to live your life from this day forward in relationship with Jesus Christ. Don't be one of the people that God says He never knew. Take the time to get to know the Lord. Sometimes we have time in our lives for everybody but God—don't let that describe your life.

Let's summarize some of the things we have learned from the Parable of the Ten Virgins and other things we have discussed so far.

- The virgins represent the spiritually pure who say they are Christians and are representative of people in the church.

- The virgins are familiar with the Word of God as represented by the Bible.

- The wise know what God has said in the Bible and then actually put that knowledge into action.

- The way the wise put their knowledge into action is by following the Holy Spirit and by doing the will of God.

- The foolish ignore the direction given in the Bible and do things their own way. They fail to cultivate a relationship with God and do what is right in their own eyes—in essence defying the will of God and cutting off the direction of the Holy Spirit.

- The foolish have alienated themselves from God to the point that He says He never knew them.

- A door is opened to the wise, a time when Jesus will gather the wise to be home with Him. The door provides a means of escape from the upcoming Day of the Lord destructions and the onslaught of the antichrist.

- The door is shut to the foolish. They will have to endure the worst period of destruction to ever come upon the earth without the protection that the Lord has focused on us in the past in the Age of Grace.

We need to do everything in our power to be counted among the wise. It's the only way you will live your life to the fullest potential God has for you.

We Need to Support Israel

There is another warning that every Christian needs to hear. We need to support the nation of Israel in every way we can. *The day that we as Americans turn away from supporting Israel is the day the Lord will turn away from the United States.*

The United States and Israel are two nations that have been linked since Israel was reborn as a nation in 1948. The US was the first vote in the United Nations in support of the formation of the nation of Israel. Harry Truman, the US President at the time, wanted to be a modern day Cyrus who returned the Jews to their homeland. Cyrus was the ancient ruler who returned the Jews to their homeland to rebuild the temple after they had been in captivity in Babylon (Isaiah 44:28). President Truman saw the same opportunity present itself in 1948 when the resolution to reestablish Israel in their homeland came to a vote in the United Nations. The United States' unwavering support ensured that Israel was reborn as a nation.

Time and time again since that time the United States has stood on the side of Israel. Our mistakes have been when we insisted that Israel needed to give away some of its land for peace, or when we have insisted on establishing a Palestinian state inside the borders of Israel. We have faced many consequences because of those actions. Now, more than ever, we need to stand firmly on the side of Israel because their situation is more precarious than it has ever been. Israel is surrounded on every side with hostile neighbors bent on their destruction.

Our focus should be on protecting Israel, not on forming nuclear arms deals with others in the Middle East—especially with countries that have no intention of honoring whatever nuclear arms deals we come up with. If a country consistently insists that the day they get nuclear weapons they will use them on Israel and the United States; then continued negotiations with that country is futility that borders on insanity.

Our fate is tied to the nation of Israel, and the following point cannot be emphasized enough: **The day the United States turns away from supporting Israel is the day the Lord will turn away from us.**

Let us all hope that day never comes.

Chapter Twenty Four

THE CONVERGENCE OF THREE SIGNS

One of the primary assertions of this book is that Israel will soon be involved in three future wars. My belief is that all of this will begin during or soon after the conclusion of the fourth Blood Moon on September 28th, 2015. A significant amount of evidence has been presented to support this conclusion.

We have also discussed the reason why these things are taking place. The Lord gave the nation of Israel a specific land grant— from the Nile River in Egypt to the Euphrates River. The nations of the world have infringed on the territory the Lord says belongs to Israel. Several nations have been set up in the land that belongs to Israel, and have embarked on almost continuous aggression toward the Jewish people. The Lord is not going to tolerate the infringement on His land grant to Israel, and the aggression against His people any longer. He will sweep the nations out of Israel's land by the hand of His people Israel in the Psalm 83 War. The Lord's land-for-peace deal will be far different than what the world has proposed. All the nations occupying area in the land set aside for Israel are going to be destroyed. The destruction they intended for the nation of Israel will be turned back upon their own heads. Israel will then occupy all the land that they have been promised.

A biblical pattern of three wars has been noted. It took three wars to destroy the nation of Israel in ancient times, and the pattern of three seems to be repeating. There have been three major wars that have secured Israel in their land up to this point in time (the War of Independence, the Six Day War, and the Yom Kippur War). We have discussed the three Blood Moon Wars, two have already taken place, and one is set to begin in the near future (the War of Independence, The Six Day War, and the upcoming Psalm 83 War). We have discussed in detail all three of the future wars (the Psalm 83 War, the Gog/Magog War, and the Battle of Armageddon).

In all of these discussions, the pattern of three keeps repeating itself. Why is that? Why is the pattern of three so important?

The reason the pattern of three is so important is because of what God has said in His Word. The Lord has consistently said "in the mouth of two or three witnesses every word may be established." (Matthew 18:16) Two witnesses are good, but three witnesses firmly establish His Word.

That's the reason we see the pattern of three in all these wars. God is firmly establishing His Word and His Will for what we are seeing happen. If the Lord allows it to happen, then there will be three witnesses that the event is going to happen to firmly establish God's Will.

In our discussion so far, we have talked about the occurrence of four Blood Moons (tetrad) on the Jewish Holy Days of Passover and Sukkot. This hadn't happened for almost five hundred years until recently during Israel's War of Independence and the Six Day War. It is happening again now, starting last year (2014) and concluding this year in September of 2015. After this year, the four Blood Moon tetrad on Jewish Holy Days will never occur again in our lifetime, or our children's lifetime, or their children's lifetime. That's how rare this event really is.

What if I were to tell you that the Blood Moon signs were not the only signs that will be given in September of 2015? What if I were to say that God is going to give two more signs in September of 2015, to firmly establish His Word with a total of three signs— so that the pattern of three is repeated even with the signs that are being given? Would that get your attention?

The pattern of three is going to be repeated even with the signs that are being given in September of 2015. The Blood Moon signs are rare—and then there are signs that are rarer still. In fact, there are some signs that are so rare that they have never been given before in the history of mankind in conjunction with each other. That is what is going to be happening in September of 2015—a convergence of three signs that have never happened before in the recorded history of our world. Needless to say, this might be a time you want to pay attention to and be especially diligent in watching what is happening around you.

The Second Sign

The second sign involves the conclusion of the Shemitah year. What exactly is the "Shemitah," and what is meant by the conclusion of the Shemitah year?

Most people are familiar with the term, the Sabbath day. In every week there are seven days, and the seventh day is considered the Sabbath day. The Sabbath day is considered sacred and was set aside as a time when people could worship the Lord and rest from their labors. What few people realize is that there was a Sabbath year also. The seventh year was considered a Sabbath year, and was referred to as the "Shemitah."

The biblical precedent for this was given in Leviticus:

"Six years thou shalt sow thy field, and six years thou shalt prune thy vineyard, and gather in the fruit thereof; but in the seventh year shall be a Sabbath of rest unto the land, a Sabbath for the Lord; thou shalt neither sow thy field, nor prune thy vineyard." (Leviticus 25:3-4)

What was supposed to happen in the seventh year, the Shemitah year? People were instructed by the Lord to cease from all their labors in their fields and vineyards and let the land rest. Whatever grew of its own in the Shemitah year was intended for the poor. The land was to have a year of rest, and the year of rest concluded on the last day of the Shemitah year. Elul was the last month of the Jewish year, and the Shemitah year concluded on the last day of Elul which is the twenty-ninth.

Not only was the land to rest, but all debts were to be canceled on the final day of the Shemitah year—Elul 29. All debtors were released from the burden of debt on the final day—and all debt related financial transactions were nullified and became void on the final day of the Shemitah year. The release of debt on the final day of the seven years was also something that was based on biblical precedent. The Lord commanded this action in His Word:

"At the end of every seven years you must cancel debts. This is how it is to be done: Every creditor shall cancel the loan he has made to his fellow Israelite. He shall not require payment from his fellow Israelite or brother, because the Lord's time for canceling debts has been proclaimed." (Deuteronomy 15:1-2 NIV)

Based on the biblical word, the Shemitah was a time of release or remission of debt. This also applied to the nullification of debt a nation acquired on a national scale. All debts and instruments of financial obligation in all realms of credit were to end on Elul 29, the final day of the Shemitah year. Everything leads up to that point, Elul 29, the culmination of the Shemitah year, when at sunset all debts were wiped out and the slate was wiped clean.

The Shemitah was instituted by God to help us remember who is in control of the world, and to remind us of the source of all of our blessings. We live in a material world where it is easy to forget about the Lord in our pursuit of gain and more and more things. God instituted the Shemitah to help us keep our focus on Him.

But what if the Shemitah year is not kept? What happens when the Shemitah is ignored and it is business as usual with no rest for the land and no cancellation of financial and credit obligations? Are there any repercussions for these transgressions from the Lord?

The Judgment of the Shemitah

The Jewish people found out precisely just how serious God is about keeping the Shemitah. While living in their Promised Land in ancient times, the nation of Israel failed to observe the Shemitah. When the nation of Israel was destroyed in 586 BC by Nebuchadnezzar, the prophets told the people that this happened because the Jewish people had failed to keep the Sabbath of years—the Shemitah.

"I will turn your cities into ruins, and lay waste your sanctuaries...I will lay waste the land...Your land will be laid waste, and your cities will lie in ruins. Then the land will enjoy its Sabbath years all the time that it lies desolate and you are in the country of your enemies; then the land will rest and enjoy its Sabbaths. All the time that is lies desolate, the land will have the rest it did not have during the Sabbaths you lived in it." (Leviticus 26:31-35 NIV)

The nation of Israel failed to observe the Shemitah, and they went into captivity for the seventy Shemitah years they had failed to observe. Only after the completion of seventy years were some of the Jews allowed to return to Jerusalem. The Jewish people learned the hard way that failure to keep this important law resulted in judgment and the loss of their nation..

What other judgments can be seen when this law is not kept? In his book, *The Mystery of the Shemitah*, Jonathan Cahn states that "the effects of the Shemitah bear key similarities to the effects of an economic and financial collapse."[28]

Peoples and nations can suffer the breakdown of their financial institutions because of the effects of the Shemitah—and the culmination of those effects happen on the last day the Shemitah year is in effect—Elul 29. Jonathan Cahn gives several examples of this in his book, and I would encourage you to read it.

For our intents and purposes, are there any examples of a manifestation of a Shemitah effect in the recent past? Are there any examples of where the financial institutions of a country have imploded to the point where the entire economic system was in danger of failure?

It's impossible to ask that question and not make a connection to our own country, the United States. Almost seven years ago, our nation teetered on the verge of total financial collapse. In September of 2008, the housing market entered the final stages of imploding in on itself, and threatened to take down all of our

---

28 Jonathan Cahn, *The Mystery of the Shemitah* (Lake Mary, FL: Front Line, 2014), p.30.

financial institutions. The two largest mortgage lenders, Fannie Mae and Freddie Mac, suffered catastrophic failure and had to be taken over by the government. The ripple effect of this meltdown caused several stalwart financial giants to go out of business. The entire economy staggered under the impact of these failures and was ready to collapse until the government intervened by pouring billions of dollars into the economy in an intervention known as Quantitative Easing.

The largest daily point drop in the history of the Dow Jones Industrial Average took place on September 29th, 2008. Stocks plunged a total of 777 points by the end of that day.[29] What few people realize is that day, September 29th, 2008, was the last day of the Shemitah year. The last day of the Shemitah year is Elul 29, and Elul 29 fell on September 29th of that particular year.

The largest point drop in the history of the Dow just happened to fall on the last day of the Shemitah year; a day set aside by the Lord for the cancellation and nullification of debt. And the amount of the point drop was impossible to ignore. It was 777 points. Seven hundred seventy seven points on the last day of the Shemitah year—a year founded on the significance of every seventh year. The Shemitah comes in the seventh year, and the last day is the culmination of the seventh year, the day when the greatest remission comes. It's absolutely mind boggling that something like this could take place and do so in a pattern reinforcing the Shemitah.

What is the message we are supposed to learn from this? It's literally as if the Lord was enforcing a Shemitah judgment on our nation three different times—7/7/7. If the largest point drop in the

---

29 Wikipedia, "List of largest daily changes in the Dow Jones Industrial Average," http://en.wikipedia.org/wiki/List_of_largest_daily_changes_in_the_Dow_Jones_Industrial_Average.

history of the Dow came on the last day of the Shemitah year on September 29th, 2008, then when was the largest point drop of the Dow before this?

As unlikely and incredible as it may seem, the largest point drop in the history of the Dow before 2008 was September 17th, 2001.[30] That just happened to be the last day of the previous Shemitah year, seven years before. If you remember, September 17th, 2001, was the day the stock market reopened after the devastation of 9/11, when our nation was allowed to be attacked, and the Twin Trade Towers came crashing down. On that day, September 17th, 2001, the Dow lost a little over 7% of its value,[31] and it came on a Shemitah year of tremendous destruction to our country.

Is this all just a coincidence? Could all of this just be a bizarre and disturbing convergence of signs with no meaning or significance attached to them? What does the Lord have to do to get our attention in these days when so many other things cry for our consideration? Will nothing awaken us from the stupor we seem to have fallen into?

The pattern of three, three witnesses to establish His Word, is manifesting even in the signs we are being given, and these signs are intensifying. Two Shemitah have manifested in September of 2001 and in 2008. Both have been devastating to the United States, and have caused the largest financial losses in the history of our country. What does the future hold in store for us on the final day the next Shemitah year? The future Shemitah year ends on Sunday, September 13th, 2015.

The Shemitah year has never concluded before in the history of mankind when a Blood Moon tetrad is manifesting. The

---

30 Wikipedia, *"List of largest daily changes in the Dow Jones Industrial Average."*
31 Wikipedia, *"List of largest daily changes in the Dow Jones Industrial Average."*

final Blood Moon is September 28th, 2015, and the last day of the Shemitah year is September 13th, 2015. These two signs manifesting in the same month is disturbing enough, and have never been seen before, but the addition of a third sign manifesting at precisely the same time as the conclusion of the 2015 Shemitah year is so mind numbing that it practically defies all reasonable explanation.

The Third Sign

The third sign will be given on the day the future Shemitah year is concluding. On September 13th, 2015, the Shemitah year concludes and there will be another sign on the very same day—a solar eclipse. Solar eclipses have always been a time that the nations of the world look on as a warning, and a time of caution. This solar eclipse will manifest in the South Polar Regions, and will be primarily visible from Antarctica. It was accompanied by a total solar eclipse that happened previously on March 20th, 2015, at the exact midpoint of the manifestation of the four Blood Moons of 2014/2015 that was primarily visible from the North Polar Regions.

It's as if the Lord is saying that He has a warning to the nations of the world that lie between the North Pole and the South Pole—that we need to pay attention and take notice of what God is going to do. *The nations that lie between the North Pole and South Pole are all the nations of the world.* The Lord is going to do something that He wants everyone to notice—and this action involves the nation of Israel.

The three signs will be given: the Blood Moons, the conclusion of the Shemitah, and the solar eclipse—all in September of 2015. These signs have never appeared together before. It's God's warning to the world. If we ignore these things, we do so at our own peril. The time of Israel's three future wars is beginning.

What Will Happen to Us?

What will happen to us when these things begin? When all of these things start happening, things are going to get messy. Let's take a best case scenario for the United States and assume that we are not going to be attacked again like we were on 9/11: that somehow the debt bubble hanging over our heads has not imploded by September of 2015; and that the stock market is still relatively strong.

If a nuclear war breaks out in the Middle East in September of 2015 or soon thereafter, the stock market will go into an absolute free fall. The market hates uncertainty, and a nuclear war in the most volatile region on the earth is the most uncertain and enigmatic scenario of all. The losses in the stock market could be the greatest we have ever seen—plunging the world and the United States into financial chaos, with no one willing or able to finance our debt. The losses in the stock market could easily surpass anything we have ever thought possible before. The unsustainable lifestyle of the United States, where we have created mountains of debt for future generations, will vanish overnight and we will be forced to live within our means.

Things will become very difficult. The best way to survive is to place your faith and trust in Jesus Christ. He is the answer when all seems hopeless, and when all you want to do is to give up. He is the light of the world, and our Rock in times of trouble. We can trust and depend on Jesus Christ.

Fifteen Days in September That Will Change the World

I've given you the best case scenario, but what scares me to death is giving you the worst case scenario. This is the thing that I did not want to write, but I felt compelled to place the following prognostication out there for all to consider. Know this, as I describe the following events, I hope with all my heart that I am wrong.

Imagine if you will the following scenario. On September 11th, 2015 the last day the stock market is open before the end of the Shemitah year, the following events begin to take place. The financial institutions of the United States are hacked and electronically attacked in a coordinated effort at the same time. Money and funds are withdrawn in a computer driven attack that drains capital at an unprecedented rate until massive amounts of money disappear. The Federal Reserve notices the anomalous activity and moves to shut down all financial transactions in our country. Before the feds can react, the damage has been done. So much money has disappeared that it will be impossible to recover.

The traders in the stock market begin to notice the unusual activity, and the stock market plunges out of control. Trading has to be halted until some semblance of order can be reestablished.

The economic institutions of the United States reel from the impact of these attacks. At least the damage has been limited because all financial transactions in our country have been halted.

This is reminiscent of the end of the Shemitah year of September, 2008, where we survived the worst economic downturn most of us have seen in our lifetime.

Then, the unthinkable happens two days later. On September 13th, 2015, the city of New York is attacked using a nuclear weapon. The epicenter of the attack is One World Trade Center, or the Freedom Tower as it has been referred to by some, the site of the 9/11 attacks in Manhattan on the Twin Towers. One World Trade Center was completed in 2013, with the last piece hoisted into place during a solar eclipse (May 10th, 2013). One World Trade Center, will be destroyed on the thirteen day of September, during another solar eclipse, and the same day the Shemitah year ends in 2015.

The time span between the financial attack on September 11th, to the nuclear attack on September 13th is three days—fulfilling the pattern of three that we have seen consistently throughout this book. The Shemitah year that ends on September 13th, 2015, is both a financial attack and a physical attack on the United States. It will be the third time the United States has suffered a Shemitah judgment, and this last one will be both an economic and physical judgment against our country.

Why in the world would the Lord ever allow something like this to happen? As the final words of this book are being written, our president has just concluded nuclear talks with Iran. By the president's own admission, and by confirmation by the nation of Iran, this deal will ultimately enable Iran to possess nuclear weapons which Iran fully intends to use on the nation of Israel. Iran has stated this fact many times. The Prime Minister of Israel, Benjamin Netanyahu, came to our country and spoke before congress imploring us not to make this deal, and yet we have insisted on making a deal that virtually insures the destruction of the nation of Israel. God will not allow the destruction of Israel, and a nuclear strike against our nation when we have virtually insured that a nuclear strike will happen against Israel may well be the reason for a Shemitah judgment against the United States.

The United States will be brought to its knees following the nuclear attack in New York. With our financial institutions in shambles, and the New York Stock Exchange destroyed, and the city of New York reeling from yet another attack, the future of the United States is uncertain. We will be unable to help Israel or any other country during this time of turmoil.

This may very well be the reason why the countries surrounding Israel decide to attack in the Psalm 83 War. The United States will be in such great chaos that any coherent response from our nation will not be forthcoming. Israel will stand on its own when the forces of the Psalm 83 coalition come against them. Knowing that a nuclear weapon has been used against the United States may make the concept of using nuclear weapons to defend itself more palatable to Israel. If they don't use their nuclear weapons, they will face certain destruction at the hands of their enemies.

The fifteen days between the Shemitah judgment of September 13th, 2015, to the time of the final manifestation of the Blood Moons on September 28th, 2015, when Israel faces almost certain attack by the Psalm 83 coalition of nations; may very well be the *Fifteen Days in September That Will Change the World.*

I hope and pray that the worst case scenario I have written above will not come to pass, and that it will business as usual during this time period. Only the Lord knows for sure.

I did not propose the worst case scenario lightly. While this book was undergoing the editing process, I went to the Lord three times in prayer for our country and asked that the worst case scenario for the United States described above be deleted from this book. At the end of the third prayer asking that our country be spared from these events, I received the following answer to my prayers in the events that took place.

The United States had just concluded nuclear talks with Iran and the president announced some of the points from the nuclear talks on Friday, April 3rd, 2015. Less than twenty-four hours later the Lord gave His response to what He thought of our nuclear deal with Iran. The third Blood Moon formed in the night skies of April 4th for all to see. The Blood Moon was clearly visible in America, just like the previous two Blood Moons. The Lord had a message He wanted America to see. The worst case scenario for the United States was left in the book and the name of this book was changed to: *Fifteen Days in September That Will Change the World.*

What Are We to Do?

The Lord is going to fulfill the land grant of the nation of Israel. The nation of Israel is going to be composed of all the lands that the Lord has given to them—regardless of the objections and raging of the nations of the world. It's going to happen because the Lord has decreed it for His Covenant People, Israel.

That's the meaning of the four Blood Moons manifesting, and the meaning of all the signs that are taking place in September of 2015. The Lord is going to start reasserting His sovereign control over the world, whether we like it or not, whether we are prepared for it or not, and whether we actively fight against Him or not.

Three signs are going to be given in September of 2015, and three wars loom on the horizon for the nation of Israel. The only thing that is going to be certain in the times of uncertainty ahead is that we are headed for times that try the very fiber in people's souls.

Chapter Twenty Five

FINAL THOUGHTS

One of the themes found throughout the Bible is that "the just shall live by faith." We find that council both in the Old and New Testaments. (Habakkuk 2:4; Romans 1:17) We have just discussed many signs that are going to be given in the near future, but I want to caution you that it is only your faith that will get you through the times that lie ahead.

This book came about through an exhaustive study of the Bible, and faith that God answers our questions through the Holy Spirit and prayer. This is a book that faith and prayer built as I searched for answers contained in the Bible. I am no prophet, and have had no special visions or revelations about what is going to happen in the future. I don't think we really need those things to figure out what the Lord wants us to know. We have God's Word, and we have just begun to plumb the depths of knowledge and insight that the Lord has placed in there for us.

I would like to say a word of caution to those that read this book. In saying what I have said I realize that God may have other plans for the start of the wars that will soon involve Israel. While many signs have been given, God cannot be restricted by anything that man will say, especially regarding the timing of when He allows things to happen. He knows things perfectly, I do not. It may very well be that nothing significant will happen in September of 2015. If that is the case, then it is because of errors in my conclusions concerning the timing of certain events. The Lord will still accomplish His will, but He will do it in accordance with His perfect knowledge. We need to be doing the things the Lord has asked us to do regardless when these events occur.

We live in a culture that has discounted God's Word. Popular books have left the impression that what God has said in the Bible cannot be trusted—and that the Bible is a haphazard collection of outdated and antiquated stories that don't have much relevance in today's sophisticated world. Yet nothing could be further from the truth. The Bible is a living and vibrant glimpse into the mind of God, with stories and examples that have as much relevance today as they have in any other time in history. History is practically jumping off the pages of God's Word in our day, with an accuracy and timeliness that is almost incomprehensible. You will learn details about what is going on in today's world with a comprehensive study of the Bible more so now than at any other time in history.

This book was written for the express purpose of letting people know that you can trust in Jesus Christ. My father is not numbered among the believers of Jesus Christ. It has always been my hope that someday he will accept Jesus as his Savior. My father is a good man who spent his life in the service of his country. He answered the call of the United States to serve as a young man, and was there throughout the years of Viet Nam and beyond.

My father's love for me was shown in the sacrifice he made for his country. Those years of service came at a price, with a cost buried deep within him that I think that I will never fathom. And yet I know that the answer he has always been searching for can be found in Jesus Christ.

This book was my attempt to reach my father and let him know that he can believe in and trust Jesus Christ. I felt that if I could write something that the Bible has told us is going to happen, but has not happened yet, then somehow his years of unbelief will fade away and he will open himself up to the only thing that brings true joy and happiness in life—a relationship with Jesus Christ.

It was that reason that I embarked on the journey of writing this impossible book. How do you write something that has not happened yet (but is contained in the Bible), with the detail and precision that God's Word provides?

To say that this is a book that faith and prayer built is a serious understatement. It was only through the guidance and direction of the Holy Spirit that I was able to put something like this together. Many times I started and the Spirit would stop me and redirect my efforts. I wrote for an entire year only to be told that I had focused on the wrong country—Israel was the country I should be focusing on, not the United States.

Time and time again I thought I had the right direction only to be led down a different path. I wasn't asking the right questions. I was focusing on the wrong things, and I was spending too much time focusing on the negative things rather than the power that God has to transform us and guide us through the dark times. I took so many missteps that I began to think I would never get it right. But then finally things began to fall into place. The patterns

God uses to accomplish His will became clear. The connections He uses in His Word began to stand out, and the promises that He has made to Israel became crystal clear to me. I don't know how I ever thought God would accomplish His will without fulfilling all of the promises He has made in His Word.

Through a slow and gradual process things began to make sense, and I began to receive less and less correction through the Holy Spirit. The importance of the wars in Israel's future, and the critical part they play in the timing of end time events became clearer. Everything began to fall into place and the book as you see it now was completed at the end of March, 2015. The impossible book was finally done; and in less than six months the events in Israel's prophetic future will begin to take place.

I have always believed that when I got this book right, it would have the power to change lives—not because of what I had done, but because it focuses on what Jesus Christ has said. I asked that this book would have the power to change the life of my father, and somehow I believe that will happen. I also believe that it has the power to change the lives of millions of people who are just like my father; good people who have never accepted Jesus Christ as their Lord and Savior. As millions accept Christ, Jesus will be glorified and many will find the peace and joy that defies understanding.

There are a few more things I need to clarify. Many who read this may think that this book is anti-Muslim. That was never the intention. I know many Muslim people and some of them are good friends. Their dedication to family and friends is admirable.

Even though I do not agree with the Muslim religion, I also recognize that radicals have hijacked their religion exploiting it for their own misguided and evil purposes. These radicals have become the vocal minority and the face of that religion.

There is a fundamental law that should be observed by the adherents of any religion. **You do not have the right in the name of any religion to go out and kill others, or force others to convert to your religion unwillingly.** If your religion can only gain converts by the force of the sword, then by the force of the sword that religion will be destroyed.

The counterfeit caliph, Gog, and the antichrist should remember this in their quest to rule the world.

A Challenge to the Reader

The biggest challenge now is getting this book out to the millions of people that can benefit from it. Time is short. The season when all of this begins is upon us. If this book has impacted you or if you know others that can benefit from the words of this book, I would like to issue you a challenge.

Let others know about this book. Buy multiple copies and give it to your friends, or buy the electronic version of the book for those who can benefit from it. There are millions of people in the world who need to know they can trust in Jesus Christ, and that the Bible is as relevant now as it has ever been. The ideas expressed in this book came directly from the Bible with the express purpose of drawing many more people to Jesus Christ.

May the Lord guide us all on our journey through life, and may He bless and keep us all.

Made in the USA
San Bernardino, CA
30 August 2015